PRAISE FOR

The Reason I Jump

"One of the most remarkable books I've ever read. It's truly
moving, eye-opening, incredibly vivid."

—JON STEWART, *The Daily Show*

"A rare road map into the world of severe autism . . .
[Higashida's] insights . . . unquestionably give those of us
whose children have autism just a little more patience, al-
lowing us to recognize the beauty in 'odd' behaviors where
perhaps we saw none."

—*People* (3½ stars)

"Small but profound . . . [Higashida's] startling, moving insights offer a rare look inside the autistic mind."

—*Parade*

"Please don't assume that *The Reason I Jump* is just another book for the crowded autism shelf. . . . This is an intimate book, one that brings readers right into an autistic mind—what it's like without boundaries of time, why cues and prompts are necessary, and why it's so impossible to hold someone else's hand. Of course, there's a wide range of behavior here; that's why 'on the spectrum' has become such a popular phrase. But by listening to this voice, we can understand its echoes."

—*Chicago Tribune* (editor's choice)

"*The Reason I Jump* is a Rosetta stone. . . . I had to keep reminding myself that the author was a thirteen-year-old boy when he wrote this . . . because the freshness of voice coexists with so much wisdom. This book takes about ninety minutes to read, and it will stretch your vision of what it is to be human."

—ANDREW SOLOMON, *The Times* (U.K.)

"Inspiring . . . surely one of the most remarkable books yet to be featured in these pages."

—*Publishers Weekly*

"[Higashida] illuminates his autism from within. . . . Anyone struggling to understand autism will be grateful for the book and translation."

—*Kirkus Reviews*

"We have our received ideas, we believe they correspond roughly to the way things are, then a book comes along that simply blows all this so-called knowledge out of the water. This is one of them . . . [*The Reason I Jump*] is an entry into another world."

—*Daily Mail* (U.K.)

"Every page dismantles another preconception about autism. . . . Once you understand how Higashida managed to write this book, you lose your heart to him."

—*New Statesman* (U.K.)

"Astonishing . . . *The Reason I Jump* builds one of the strongest bridges yet constructed between the world of autism and the neurotypical world. . . . There are many more questions I'd like to ask Naoki, but the first words I'd say to him are 'thank you.'"

—*The Sunday Times* (U.K.)

"Like millions of parents confronted with autism, Mitchell and his wife found themselves searching for answers and finding few that were satisfactory. Help, when it arrived, came not from some body of research but from the writings of a Japanese schoolboy, Naoki Higashida. *The Reason I Jump* . . . is a book that acts like a door to another logic, explaining why an autistic child might flap his hands in front of his face, disappear suddenly from home—or jump."

—*The Telegraph* (U.K.)

"Whether or not you have experienced raising a child who is autistic . . . this little book, which packs immeasurable honesty and truth into its pages, will simply detonate any illusions, assumptions, and conclusions you've made about the condition. . . . What Higashida has done by communicating his reality is to offer carers a way forward and offer teachers new ways of working with the children, and thus opening up and expanding the possibilities for autistic kids to feel less alone. All that in less than 200 pages? What an accomplishment."

—*The Herald* (Dublin)

"*The Reason I Jump* is a wise, beautiful, intimate and courageous explanation of autism as it is lived every day by one remarkable boy. Naoki Higashida takes us 'behind the mirror'—his testimony should be read by parents, teachers, siblings, friends, and anybody who knows and loves an autistic person. I only wish I'd had this book to defend myself when I was Naoki's age."

—TIM PAGE, author of *Parallel Play* and
professor of journalism and music at
the University of Southern California

The Reason I Jump

The Reason I Jump

THE INNER VOICE OF A
THIRTEEN-YEAR-OLD BOY WITH AUTISM

Naoki Higashida

Translated by KA Yoshida and David Mitchell

RANDOM HOUSE

New York

2016 Random House Trade Paperback Edition

Published in the United States by Random House,
an imprint and division of Penguin Random House LLC, New York.

RANDOM HOUSE and the HOUSE colophon are
registered trademarks of Penguin Random House LLC.

Originally published in Japan in Japanese by Escor Publishers Ltd. in 2007. This
translation was originally published in the United Kingdom by Sceptre, an imprint of
Hodder & Stoughton, an Hachette UK Company, and in Canada by Alfred A. Knopf
Canada, a division of Random House of Canada Limited, in 2013.
Originally published in hardcover in the United States by Random House,
an imprint and division of Penguin Random House LLC, in 2013.
The interview between David Mitchell and Andrew Solomon
was originally published in *The Guardian*.

This book contains an excerpt from the forthcoming book
Fall Down 7 Times Get Up 8 by Naoki Higashida. This excerpt has been set for this
edition only and may not reflect the final content of the forthcoming edition.

LIBRARY OF CONGRESS CATALOGING-IN-PUBLICATION DATA
Higashida, Naoki.
[Jiheisho no boku ga tobihaneru riyu. English]The reason I jump /
by Naoki Higashida ; translated by KA Yoshida and David Mitchell.
pages cm
ISBN 978-0-8129-8515-3
eBook ISBN 978-0-8129-9487-2
1. Higashida, Naoki, 1992– 2. Autistic people—Japan—Biography.
3. Autistic people—Psychology. 4. Autism. I. Title.
RC553.A88H5313 2013   616.85'8820092—dc23
[B] 2012045703

Printed in the United States of America on acid-free paper
randomhousebooks.com

12 14 16 18 19 17 15 13

Book design by Donna Sinisgalli

Introduction

DAVID MITCHELL

—

The thirteen-year-old author of this book invites you, his reader, to imagine a daily life in which your faculty of speech is taken away. Explaining that you're hungry, or tired, or in pain, is now as beyond your powers as a chat with a friend. I'd like to push the thought-experiment a little further. Now imagine that after you lose your ability to communicate, the editor-in-residence who orders your thoughts walks out without notice. The chances are that you never knew this mind-editor existed, but now that he or she has gone, you realize too late how the editor allowed your mind to function for all these years. A dam-burst of ideas, memories, impulses and thoughts is cascading over you, unstoppably. Your editor controlled this flow, diverting the vast majority away, and recommending just a tiny number for your conscious consideration. But now you're on your own.

Now your mind is a room where twenty radios, all tuned to different stations, are blaring out voices and music. The radios have no off-switches or volume controls, the room you're in has no door or window, and relief will come only when you're too exhausted to stay awake. To make matters worse, another hitherto unrecognized editor has just quit without notice—your editor of the senses. Suddenly sensory input from your environment is flooding in too, unfiltered in quality and overwhelming in quantity. Colors and patterns swim and clamor for your attention. The fabric softener in your sweater smells as strong as air freshener fired up your nostrils. Your comfy jeans are now as scratchy as steel wool. Your vestibular and proprioceptive senses are also out of kilter, so the floor keeps tilting like a ferry in heavy seas, and you're no longer sure where your hands and feet are in relation to the rest of you. You can feel the plates of your skull, plus your facial muscles and your jaw; your head feels trapped inside a motorcycle helmet three sizes too small which may or may not explain why the air conditioner is as deafening as an electric drill, but your father—who's right here in front of you—sounds as if he's speaking to you from a cellphone, on a train going through lots of short tunnels, in fluent Cantonese. You are no longer able to comprehend your mother tongue, or any tongue: from now on, all languages will be foreign languages. Even your sense of time has gone, rendering you unable to distinguish between a minute and an hour, as if you've been entombed in an Emily Dickinson poem about eternity, or locked into a time-bending SF film. Poems and films, however, come to an end, whereas this is your new ongoing reality. Autism is a lifelong condition. But even the word "autism" makes no more sense to you now than the word 自閉症 or αυτισμός or ऑटिज़्म.

Thanks for sticking to the end, though the real end, for most of us, would involve sedation and being forcibly hospitalized, and what happens next it's better not to speculate. Yet for those people born onto the autistic spectrum, this unedited, unfiltered and scary-as-all-hell reality is home. The functions that genetics bestows on the rest of us—the "editors"—as a birthright, people with autism must spend their lives learning how to simulate. It is an intellectual and emotional task of Herculean, Sisyphean and Titanic proportions, and if the autistic people who undertake it aren't heroes, then I don't know what heroism is, never mind that the heroes have no choice. Sentience itself is not so much a fact to be taken for granted, but a brick-by-brick, self-built construct requiring constant maintenance. As if this wasn't a tall enough order, people with autism must survive in an outside world where "special needs" is playground slang for "retarded," where meltdowns and panic attacks are viewed as tantrums, where disability allowance claimants are assumed by many to be welfare scroungers, and where British foreign policy can be described as "autistic" by a French minister. (M. Lellouche apologized later, explaining that he never dreamed that the adjective could have caused offense. I don't doubt it.)

Autism is no cakewalk for the child's parents or carers either, and raising an autistic son or daughter is no job for the fainthearted—in fact, faintheartedness is doomed by the first niggling doubt that there's Something Not Quite Right about your sixteen-month-old. On Diagnosis Day, a child psychologist hands down the verdict with a worn-smooth truism about your son still being the same little guy that he was before this life-redefining news was confirmed. Then you run the gauntlet of other people's reactions: "It's just so sad"; "What, so he's going to be like Dustin Hoffman in *Rain Man*?"; "I hope you're not going to take this so-called 'diagnosis' lying down!"; and my favorite, "Yes, well, I told my pediatrician where to go stick his MMR jabs." Your first contacts with most support agencies will put the last nails in the coffin of faintheartedness, and graft onto you a layer of scar tissue and cynicism as thick as rhino hide. There are gifted and resourceful people working in autism support, but with depressing regularity government policy appears to be about Band-Aids and fig leaves, and not about realizing the potential of children with special needs and helping them become long-term net contributors to society. The scant silver lining is that medical theory is no longer blaming your wife for causing the autism by being a "Refrigerator Mother" as it did not so long ago (Refrigerator Fathers were unavailable for comment) and that you don't live in a society where people with autism are believed to be witches or devils and get treated accordingly.

Where to turn to next? Books. (You'll have started already, because the first reaction of friends and family desperate to help is to send clippings, Web links and literature, however tangential to your own situation.) Special Needs publishing is a jungle. Many *How to Help Your Autistic Child* manuals have a doctrinaire spin, with generous helpings of © and ™. They may contain usable ideas, but reading them can feel depressingly like being asked to join a political party or a church. The more academic texts are denser, more cross-referenced and rich in pedagogy and abbreviations. Of course it's good that academics are researching the field, but often the gap between the theory and what's unraveling on your kitchen floor is too wide to bridge.

Another category is the more confessional memoir,

usually written by a parent, describing the impact of autism on the family and sometimes the positive effect of an unorthodox treatment. These memoirs are media-friendly and raise the profile of autism in the marketplace of worthy causes, but I have found their practical use to be limited, and in fairness they usually aren't written to be useful. Every autistic person exhibits his or her own variation of the condition—autism is more like retina patterns than measles—and the more unorthodox the treatment for one child, the less likely it is to help another (mine, for example).

A fourth category of autism book is the "autism autobiography" written by insiders on the autistic spectrum, the most famous example being *Thinking in Pictures* by Temple Grandin. For sure, these books are often illuminating, but almost by definition they tend to be written by adults who have already worked things out, and they couldn't help me where I needed help most: to understand why my three-year-old was banging his head against the floor; or flapping his fingers in front of his eyes at high speed; or suffering from skin so sensitive that he couldn't sit or lie down; or howling with grief for forty-five minutes when the *Pingu* DVD was too scratched for the DVD player to read it. My reading provided theories, angles, anecdotes and guesses about these challenges, but without reasons all I could do was look on, helplessly.

One day my wife received a remarkable book she had ordered from Japan called *The Reason I Jump*. Its author, Naoki Higashida, was born in 1992 and was still in junior high school when the book was published. Naoki's autism is severe enough to make spoken communication pretty much impossible, even now. But thanks to an ambitious teacher and his own persistence, he learned to spell out words directly onto an alphabet grid. A Japanese alphabet grid is a table of the basic forty Japanese hiragana letters, and its English counterpart is a copy of the QWERTY keyboard, drawn onto a card and laminated. Naoki communicates by pointing to the letters on these grids to spell out whole words, which a helper at his side then transcribes. These words build up into sentences, paragraphs and entire books. "Extras" around the side of the grids include numbers, punctuation, and the words FINISHED, YES and NO. (Although Naoki can also write and blog directly onto a computer via its keyboard, he finds the lower-tech alphabet grid a "steadier handrail" as it offers fewer distractions and helps him to focus.) Even in primary school this method enabled him to communicate with others, and compose poems and story books, but it was his explanations about why children with autism do what they do that were, literally, the answers that we had been waiting for. Composed by a writer still with one foot in childhood, and whose autism was at least as challenging and life-altering as our son's, *The Reason I Jump* was a revelatory godsend. Reading it felt as if, for the first time, our own son was talking to us about what was happening inside his head, through Naoki's words.

The book goes much further than providing information, however: it offers up proof that locked inside the helpless-seeming autistic body is a mind as curious, subtle and complex as yours, as mine, as anyone's. During the 24/7 grind of being a carer, it's all too easy to forget the fact that the person you're doing so much for is, and is obliged to be, more resourceful than you in many respects. As the months turn into years "forgetting" can become "disbelieving," and this lack of faith makes both the carer and the cared-for vulnerable to negativities. Naoki Higashida's gift is to restore faith: by demonstrating intellectual acuity and spiritual curiosity; by analysis of his environment and his condition; and by a puckish sense of humor and a drive to write fiction. We're not talking signs or hints of these mental propensities: they're already here, in the book which (I hope) you're about to read.

If that weren't enough, *The Reason I Jump* unwittingly

discredits the doomiest item of received wisdom about autism—that people with autism are antisocial loners who lack empathy with others. Naoki Higashida reiterates repeatedly that no, he values the company of other people very much. But because communication is so fraught with problems, a person with autism tends to end up alone in a corner, where people then see him or her and think, *Aha, classic sign of autism, that.* Similarly, if people with autism are oblivious to other people's feelings, how could Naoki testify that the most unendurable aspect of autism is the knowledge that he makes other people stressed out and depressed? How could he write a story (entitled "I'm Right Here" and included at the end of the book) boasting characters who display a range of emotions and a plot designed to tweak the tear glands? Like all storytelling mammals, Naoki is anticipating his audience's emotions and manipulating them. That is empathy. The conclusion is that both emotional poverty and an aversion to company are not *symptoms* of autism but *consequences* of autism, its harsh lockdown on self-expression and society's near-pristine ignorance about what's happening inside autistic heads.

For me, all the above is transformative, life-enhancing knowledge. When you know that your kid wants to speak with you, when you know that he's taking in his surroundings every bit as attentively as your nonautistic daughter, whatever the evidence to the contrary, then you can be ten times more patient, willing, understanding and communicative; and ten times better able to help his development. It is no exaggeration to say that *The Reason I Jump* allowed me to round a corner in our relationship with our son. Naoki Higashida's writing administered the kick I needed to stop feeling sorry for myself, and start thinking how much tougher life was for my son, and what I could do to make it less tough. Virtuous spirals are as wonderful in special-needs parenting as anywhere else: your expectations for your child are raised; your stamina to get through the rocky patches is strengthened; and your child senses this, and responds. My wife began to work on an informal translation of Naoki's book into English so that our son's other carers and tutors could read it, as well as a few friends who also have sons and daughters with autism in our corner of Ireland. But after discovering through Web groups that other expat Japanese mothers of children with autism were frustrated by the lack of a translation into English, we began to wonder if there might not be a much wider audience for Naoki Higashida. This English translation of *The Reason I Jump* is the result.

The author is not a guru, and if the answers to a few of the questions may seem a little sparse, remember he was only thirteen when he wrote them. Even when he can't provide a short, straight answer—such as to the question "Why do you like lining up your toys so obsessively?"— what he has to say is still worthwhile. Naoki Higashida has continued to write, keeps a nearly daily blog, has become well known in autism advocacy circles and has been featured regularly in the Japanese *Big Issue*. He says that he aspires to be a writer, but it's obvious to me that he already is one—an honest, modest, thoughtful writer, who has won over enormous odds and transported first-hand knowledge from the severely autistic mind into the wider world; a process as taxing for him as, say, the act of carrying water in cupped palms across a bustling Times Square or Piccadilly Circus would be to you or me. The three characters used for the word "autism" in Japanese signify "self," "shut" and "illness." My imagination converts these characters into a prisoner locked up and forgotten inside a solitary confinement cell waiting for someone, anyone, to realize he or she is in there. *The Reason I Jump* knocks out a brick in the wall.

The Reason I Jump

Preface

When I was small, I didn't even know that I was a kid with special needs. How did I find out? By other people telling me that I was different from everyone else, and that this was a problem. True enough. It was very hard for me to act like a normal person, and even now I still can't "do" a real conversation. I have no problem reading books aloud and singing, but as soon as I try to speak with someone, my words just vanish. Sure, sometimes I manage a few words—but even these can come out the complete opposite of what I want to say! I can't respond appropriately when I'm told to do something, and whenever I get nervous I run off from wherever I happen to be. So even a straightforward activity like shopping can be really challenging if I'm tackling it on my own.

So *why* can't I do these things? During my frustrating, miserable, helpless days, I've started imagining what it would be like if everyone was autistic. If autism was regarded simply as a personality type, things would be so much easier and happier for us than they are now. For sure, there are bad times when we cause a lot of hassle for other people, but what we really want is to be able to look toward a brighter future.

Thanks to training I've had with Ms. Suzuki at Hagukumi School, and my mom, I've learned a method of communication via writing. Now I can even write on my computer. Problem is, many children with autism don't have the means to express themselves, and often even their own parents don't have a clue what they might be thinking. So my big hope is that I can help a bit by explaining, in my own way, what's going on in the minds of people with autism. I also hope that, by reading this book, you might become a better friend of someone with autism.

You can't judge a person by their looks. But once you know the other person's inner self, both of you can be that much closer. From your point of view, the world of autism must look like a deeply mysterious place. So please, spare a little time to listen to what I have to say.

And have a nice trip through our world.

Naoki Higashida
Japan, 2006

はい ◎　取消し　✕　いいえ

Q W E R T Y U I O P

A S D F G H J K L

Z X C V B N M　　　?

0 1 2 3 4 5 6 7 8 9 10

田 「 」（ ）行　田　おわり

あいうえお
かきくけこ　　🔲
さしすせそ　　🔲
たちってと
なにぬねの　　🔲🔲🔲
はひふへほ
まみむめも　　、
やゆよ　　　　。
らりるれろ
わをん
0 1 2 3 4 5 6 7 8 9 10

Q1 *How are you writing these sentences?*

The alphabet grid is a method of non-vocal communication. You might think that speech is the only way to get your points and intentions across, but there is another way to say what you want without using the vocal nervous system. At first I never dreamed I could make it work, but now I'm well able to express my true self using only a computer and an alphabet grid.

This was an incredible feeling! Not being able to talk means not being able to share what you're feeling and thinking. It's like being a doll spending your whole life in isolation, without dreams and without hopes. Sure, it took a long time before I could finally start communicating via written text on my own, but on that first day when my mom supported my writing hand in hers, I began to acquire a new way of interacting with others.

Then, to allow more independent communication, Mom invented the alphabet grid. The alphabet grid makes it possible to form my words by simply pointing to their letters, instead of having to write them out one by one. This also lets me anchor my words, words that would otherwise flutter off as soon as I tried to speak them.

Often, while I was learning this method, I'd feel utterly beaten. But finally I arrived at the point where I could indicate the letters by myself. What kept me hammering away at it was the thought that to live my life as a human being, nothing is more important than being able to express myself. So for me, the alphabet grid isn't just about putting together sentences: it's about getting across to other people what I want and need them to understand.

People often tell me that when I'm talking to myself my voice is really loud, even though I still can't say what I need to, and even though my voice at other times is way too soft. This is one of those things I can't control. It really gets me down. Why can't I fix it?

When I'm talking in a weird voice, I'm not doing it on purpose. Sure, there are some times when I find the sound of my own voice comforting, when I'll use familiar words or easy-to-say phrases. But the voice I can't control is different. This one blurts out, not because I want it to; it's more like a reflex.

A reflex reacting to what? To what I've just seen, in some cases, or to some old memories. When my weird voice gets triggered, it's almost impossible to hold it back—and if I try, it actually hurts, almost as if I'm strangling my own throat.

I'd be okay with my weird voice on my own, but I'm aware that it bothers other people. How often have the strange sounds coming out of my mouth embarrassed me nearly to death? Honest, I want to be nice and calm and quiet too! But even if we're ordered to keep our mouths shut or to be quiet, we simply don't know how. Our voices are like our breathing, I feel, just coming out of our mouths, unconsciously.

Q3 *Why do you ask the same questions over and over?*

It's true; I always ask the same questions. "What day is it today?" or "Is it a school day tomorrow?" Simple matters like these, I ask again and again. I don't repeat my question because I didn't understand—in fact, even as I'm asking, I know I do understand.

The reason why? Because I very quickly forget what it is I've just heard. Inside my head there really isn't such a big difference between what I was told just now, and what I heard a long, long time ago.

So I do understand things, but my way of remembering them works differently from everyone else's. I imagine a normal person's memory is arranged continuously, like a line. My memory, however, is more like a pool of dots. I'm always "picking up" these dots—by asking my questions— so I can arrive back at the memory that the dots represent.

But there's another reason for our repeated questioning: it lets us play with words. We aren't good at conversation, and however hard we try, we'll never speak as effortlessly as you do. The big exception, however, is words or phrases we're very familiar with. Repeating these is great fun. It's like a game of catch with a ball. Unlike the words we're ordered to say, repeating questions we already know the answers to can be a pleasure—it's playing with sound and rhythm.

Q4 *Why do you echo questions back at the asker?*

For a long time, I've noticed that people with autism often repeat questions, like parrots. Instead of answering the question, we just say the exact same question straight back at the person asking it. Once, I thought we did it simply because we didn't know how to answer, but now I think there's more to the mystery than this.

Firing the question back is a way of sifting through our memories to pick up clues about what the questioner is asking. We understand the question okay, but we can't answer it until we fish out the right "memory picture" in our heads.

It's quite a complicated process, this. First, I scan my memory to find an experience closest to what's happening now. When I've found a good close match, my next step is to try to recall what I said at that time. If I'm lucky, I hit upon a usable experience and all is well. If I'm not lucky, I get clobbered by the same sinking feeling I had originally, and I'm unable to answer the question I'm being asked. No matter how hard I try to stop it, that weird voice slips out, making me more flustered and discouraged, and so it gets harder and harder to say anything.

In "set-pattern" conversations, we manage much better; although, of course, when it comes to talking about your feelings, these patterns are no use at all. In fact, by relying on them too much you can end up saying the opposite of what you wanted to say. I swear conversation is such hard work! To make myself understood, it's like I have to speak in an unknown foreign language, every minute of every day.

Q5 *Why do you do things you shouldn't even when you've been told a million times not to?*

"How many *times* do I have to *tell* you?!"

Us people with autism hear that all the time. Me, I'm always being told off for doing the same old things. It may look as if we're being bad out of naughtiness, but honestly, we're not. When we're being told off, we feel terrible that yet again we've done what we've been told not to. But when the chance comes once more, we've pretty much forgotten about the last time and we just get carried away yet again. It's as if something that isn't us is urging us on.

You must be thinking: "Is he *never* going to learn?" We know we're making you sad and upset, but it's as if we don't have any say in it, I'm afraid, and that's the way it is. But please, whatever you do, don't give up on us. We need your help.

Q6 *Do you find childish language easier to understand?*

Children with autism are also growing and developing every single day, yet we are forever being treated like babies. I guess this is because we seem to act younger than our true age, but whenever anyone treats me as if I'm still a toddler, it really hacks me off. I don't know whether people think I'll understand baby-language better, or whether they think I just prefer being spoken to in that way.

I'm not asking you to deliberately use difficult language when you talk to people with autism—just that you treat us as we are, according to our age. Every single time I'm talked down to, I end up feeling utterly miserable—as if I'm being given zero chance of a decent future.

True compassion is about not bruising the other person's self-respect. That's what I think, anyway.

Q7 *Why do you speak in that peculiar way?*

Sometimes, people with autism speak with a strange intonation, or use language in a different way. Non-autistic people can sort out what they want to say in real time, while they're having their conversation. But in our case, the words we want to say and the words we *can* say don't always match that well. Which is why our speech can sound a bit odd, I guess. When there's a gap between what I'm thinking and what I'm saying, it's because the words coming out of my mouth are the only ones I can access at that time. These words are either available because I'm always using them or because they left a lasting impression on me at some point in the past.

Some of you may think we read aloud with a strange intonation, too. This is because we can't read the story and imagine the story at the same time. Just the act of reading costs us a lot of effort—sorting out the words and somehow voicing them is already a very tall order.

More practice will help, however. Please never laugh at us, even when we're doing a less than great job.

Q8 *Why do you take ages to answer questions?*

You normal people, you talk at an incredible speed. Between thinking something in your head and saying it takes you just a split second. To us, that's like magic!

So is there something wrong with the circuitry in our brains? Life's been tough for people with autism, pretty much forever, yet nobody's really been able to identify the causes of autism. For sure, it takes us ages to respond to what the other person has just said. The reason we need so much time isn't necessarily because we haven't understood, but because by the time it's our turn to speak, the reply we wanted to make has often upped and vanished from our heads.

I don't know if this is making a whole lot of sense to you. Once our reply has disappeared, we can never get it back again. *What did he say again? How was I going to answer her question?* . . . Search me! And all the while, we're being bombarded by yet more questions. I end up thinking, *This is just hopeless.* It's as if I'm drowning in a flood of words.

Making sounds with your mouth isn't the same thing as communication, right? Lots of people can't get their heads fully around this, I think. Isn't there a belief out there that if a person is using verbal language, it follows that the person is saying what they want to say? It's thanks to this belief that those of us with autism get even more locked up inside ourselves.

Just because some of us can make sounds or utter words, it doesn't follow automatically that what we've said is really what we wanted to say. Even with straightforward "Yes" or "No" questions, we make mistakes. It happens all the time to me that the other person misunderstands or misinterprets what I've just said.

Because I'm barely able to hold a conversation, fixing what's gone wrong is beyond my powers. Every time this happens, I end up hating myself for being so useless and clamming up. Please don't assume that every single word we say is what we intended. This makes communication between us difficult, I know—we can't even use gestures—but we really badly want you to understand what's going on inside our hearts and minds. And basically, my feelings are pretty much the same as yours.

Q10 *Why can't you have a proper conversation?*

For a long time I've been wondering why us people with autism can't talk properly. I can never say what I really want to. Instead, verbal junk that hasn't got anything to do with anything comes pouring out of my mouth. This used to get me down badly, and I couldn't help envying all those people who speak without even trying. Our feelings are the same as everyone else's, but we can't find a way to express them.

We don't even have proper control over our own bodies. Both staying still and moving when we're told to are tricky—it's as if we're remote-controlling a faulty robot. On top of this, we're always getting told off, and we can't even explain ourselves. I used to feel abandoned by the whole world.

Please don't judge us from the outside only. I don't know why we can't talk properly. But it's not that we won't talk—it's that we can't talk and we're suffering because of it. All on our own, there's nothing we can do about this problem, and there were times when I used to wonder why Non-Speaking Me had ever been born. But having started with text communication, now I'm able to express myself via the alphabet grid and a computer, and being able to share what I think allows me to understand that I, too, exist in this world as a human being.

Can you imagine how your life would be if you couldn't talk?

The Mystery of the Missing Words

———

Us kids with autism, we never use enough words, and it's these missing words that can cause all the trouble. In this example, three friends are talking about their classmate who has autism:

"Hey, she just said, 'All of us'!"

"So . . . that must mean she wants to join in with us, yeah?"

"Dunno. Maybe she wants to know if we're all doing it."

In fact, the autistic girl's 'all of us' came from something the teacher had said earlier on in the day: "Tomorrow, all of us are going to the park." What the girl wanted to find out was *when* they were going. She tried to do this by repeating the only words she could use, "all of us." Here you can see how our missing words tweak your imaginations and send you off on wild-goose chases, here, there and everywhere.

Honestly, what a mysterious language us kids with autism speak!

Q11 *Why don't you make eye contact when you're talking?*

True, we don't look at people's eyes very much. "Look whoever you're talking with properly in the eye," I've been told, again and again and again, but I still can't do it. To me, making eye contact with someone I'm talking to feels a bit creepy, so I tend to avoid it.

Then where exactly am I looking? You might well suppose that we're just looking down, or at the general background. But you'd be wrong. What we're actually looking at is the other person's voice. Voices may not be visible things, but we're trying to listen to the other person with all of our sense organs. When we're fully focused on working out what the heck it is you're saying, our sense of sight sort of zones out. If you can't make out what you're seeing, it's the same as not seeing anything at all.

What's bothered me for a long time is this idea people have that so long as we're keeping eye contact while they're talking to us, that alone means we're taking in every word. Ha! If only that was all it took, my disability would have been cured a long, long time ago . . .

Q12 *You seem to dislike holding hands with people.*

It's not that we don't like holding hands, it's just that, if we happen to spot something interesting, we can't help but dash off and let go of the hand we were holding. I don't even remember letting it go until I hear the other person say, "Huh—it looks like he doesn't want to hold my hand."

That really used to depress me. But because I can't explain to the person why I let go of his or her hand, and since I do in fact find it hard to keep holding the hand for long, there's not much I can do about the misunderstanding.

It's really not a matter of whose hand I'm holding, or even of the act of holding hands itself. It's this impulse kids with autism have to dart off to anything that looks remotely interesting: this is what we have to tackle.

Q13 *Do you prefer to be on your own?*

"Ah, don't worry about him—he'd rather be on his own."

How many times have we heard this? I can't believe that anyone born as a human being really wants to be left all on their own, not really. No, for people with autism, what we're anxious about is that we're causing trouble for the rest of you, or even getting on your nerves. *This* is why it's hard for us to stay around other people. This is why we often end up being left on our own.

The truth is, we'd love to be with other people. But because things never, ever go right, we end up getting used to being alone, without even noticing this is happening. Whenever I overhear someone remark how much I prefer being on my own, it makes me feel desperately lonely. It's as if they're deliberately giving me the cold-shoulder treatment.

If someone's talking to me from somewhere far off, I don't notice. You're probably thinking, "Same here," yes? A major headache for me, however, is that even when someone's right here in front of me, I still don't notice when they're talking to me.

"Not noticing," however, is not the same as "deliberately ignoring." But often people assume I must be arrogant or "retarded." People around me always make me realize that I'm being spoken to by saying things like, "Say hello back, then, Naoki," or, "What do you say, then?" So whenever that happens I just repeat what I've been told to say, like a mynah bird learning a new word. Even though I feel guilty toward the person who has spoken to me, I can't even apologize, so I end up feeling miserable and ashamed that I can't manage a proper human relationship.

A person who's looking at a mountain far away doesn't notice the prettiness of a dandelion in front of them. A person who's looking at a dandelion in front of them doesn't see the beauty of a mountain far away. To us, people's voices are a bit like that. It's very difficult for us to know someone's there and that they're talking to us, just by their voice.

So it would help us a great deal if you could just use our names first to get our attention, before you start talking to us.

Q15 *Why are your facial expressions so limited?*

Our expressions only seem limited because you think differently from us. It's troubled me for quite a while that I can't laugh along when everyone else is laughing. For a person with autism, the idea of what's fun or funny doesn't match yours, I guess. More than that, there are times when situations feel downright hopeless to us—our daily lives are so full of tough stuff to tackle. At other times, if we're surprised, or feel tense, or embarrassed, we just freeze up and become unable to show any emotion whatsoever.

Criticizing people, winding them up, making idiots of them or fooling them doesn't make people with autism laugh. What makes us smile from the inside is seeing something beautiful, or a memory that makes us laugh. This generally happens when there's nobody watching us. And at night, on our own, we might burst out laughing underneath the duvet, or roar with laughter in an empty room . . . when we don't need to think about other people or anything else, that's when we wear our natural expressions.

Q16 *Is it true that you hate being touched?*

Personally, I have no particular problem with physical contact, but sure, some people with autism can't stand being hugged or touched. I don't know why, to be honest—I guess it just makes them feel uneasy. Even the way we adjust our clothing to match the season, putting on more clothes in winter and fewer in summertime, this can be a very big deal for people with tactile issues. Acting accordingly as situations change is a tough call.

More generally, for a person with autism, being touched by someone else means that the toucher is exercising control over the person's body, which not even its owner can control properly. It's as if we lose who we are. Think about it—that's terrifying!

There's also the dread that by being touched our thoughts will become visible. And if that happened, the other person would *really* start worrying about us. You see? We put up a barricade around ourselves to keep people out.

Q17 *Why do you wave goodbye with your palm facing yourself?*

When I was small, I used to wave goodbye with my palm facing inward when I was told, "Wave bye-bye!" I found simple gym exercises and dancing quite impossible. The reason is that imitating movement is difficult for people with autism. Because we don't know our own body parts so well, moving those parts of the body we can track with our eyes is our first step toward imitating movement properly.

I never understood people when they told me that I was waving goodbye the wrong way around, until one day I saw myself in a full-length mirror. That was when I realized—I was waving goodbye to myself!

Slip Sliding Away

"I can run faster than any of us!" said the Hare, boinging away.

"But we had a race a long time ago to settle this and I won," said the Tortoise, crossly. "I'm the fastest."

None of the other animals was at all interested. "Ah, who cares?"

But the Hare insisted on having another race, so the Tortoise finally gave in and turned up at the starting line.

The race between the Hare and the Tortoise was about to start.

"Ready, set, go!"

The Hare dashed away at terrific speed.

The Tortoise slipped and flipped over onto his back, at which all the other animals ran up to the Tortoise to see if he was all right: "Poor you, are you okay? You'd better go home and rest."

And so they all carried the Tortoise back to his house.

The Hare reached the finish line.

Nobody was waiting but himself.

Q18 *When you're on one of your highs, what's going through your mind?*

Sometimes people with autism start laughing like a hyena or appear to be having enormous fun on their own without any obvious reason for it. You must be wondering, *What on Earth's gotten into him?*

At times like these, we're having "imaginings." Or not quite imaginings, but we experience pictures or scenes in our minds that pop up out of nowhere. Maybe it's the memory of something that made us laugh, or maybe it's a page from a book we read.

This might be hard for you to understand. But try to see these "highs" as a stronger version of those times when you remember something funny and can't help but chuckle about it.

Q19 *What are your flashback memories like?*

We do remember what we did, when, where, who we did it with and things like this, but these memories are all scattershot and never connected in the right order. The trouble with scattered memories is that sometimes they replay themselves in my head as if they had only just taken place—and when this happens, the emotions I felt originally all come rushing back to me, like a sudden storm. This is a flashback memory.

I know I have lots of pleasant memories, but my flashback memories are always bad ones, and from out of the blue I get incredibly distressed, burst into tears or just start panicking. Never mind that it's a memory from ages ago— the same helpless feeling I had then overflows and floods out and it just won't stop.

So when this happens, just let us have a good cry, and then we can get back onto our feet. Maybe the racket we make will get on your nerves a bit, but please try to understand what we're going through, and stay with us.

Q20 *Why do you make a huge fuss over tiny mistakes?*

When I see I've made a mistake, my mind shuts down. I cry, I scream, I make a huge fuss, and I just can't think straight about anything anymore. However tiny the mistake, for me it's a massive deal, as if Heaven and Earth have been turned upside down. For example, when I pour water into a glass, I can't stand it if I spill even a drop.

It must be hard for you to understand why this could make me so unhappy. And even to me, I know really that it's not such a big deal. But it's almost impossible for me to keep my emotions contained. Once I've made a mistake, the fact of it starts rushing toward me like a tsunami. And then, like trees or houses being destroyed by the tsunami, I get destroyed by the shock. I get swallowed up in the moment, and can't tell the right response from the wrong response. All I know is that I have to get out of the situation as soon as I can, so I don't drown. To get away, I'll do anything. Crying, screaming and throwing things, hitting out even . . .

Finally, finally, I'll calm down and come back to myself. Then I see no sign of the tsunami attack—only the wreckage I've made. And when I see that, I hate myself. I just hate myself.

Q21 *Why don't you do what you're told right away?*

There are times when I can't do what I want to, or what I have to. It doesn't mean I don't want to do it. I just can't get it all together, somehow. Even performing one straightforward task, I can't get started as smoothly as you can. Here's how I have to go about things:

1. I think about what I'm going to do.
2. I visualize how I'm going to do it.
3. I encourage myself to get going.

How smoothly I can do the job depends on how smoothly this process goes.

There are times when I can't act, even though I really, badly want to. This is when my body is beyond my control. I don't mean I'm ill or anything. It's as if my whole body, except for my soul, feels as if it belongs to somebody else and I have zero control over it. I don't think you could ever imagine what an agonizing sensation this is.

You can't always tell just by looking at people with autism, but we never really feel that our bodies are our own. They're always acting up and going outside our control. Stuck inside them, we're struggling so hard to make them do what we tell them.

Q22 *Do you hate it when we make you do things?*

Us kids with autism would like you to watch out for us—meaning, "Please never give up on us." The reason I say "watch out for us" is that we can be made stronger just by the fact you're watching.

Just going by how we respond, it's difficult for you to tell if we've understood what you're saying or not. And often we still can't do something however often you've shown us how to do it.

That's just the way we are. On our own we simply don't know how to get things done the same way you do them. But, like everyone else, we want to do the best we possibly can. When we sense you've given up on us, it makes us feel miserable. So please keep helping us, through to the end.

Q23 *What's the worst thing about having autism?*

You never notice. Really, you have no idea quite how miserable we are. The people who are looking after us may say, "Minding these kids is *really* hard work, you know!" but for us—who are always causing the problems and are useless at pretty much everything we try to do—you can't begin to imagine how miserable and sad we get.

Whenever we've done something wrong, we get told off or laughed at, without even being able to apologize, and we end up hating ourselves and despairing about our own lives, again and again and again. It's impossible not to wonder why we were born into this world as human beings at all.

But I ask you, those of you who are with us all day, not to stress yourselves out because of us. When you do this, it feels as if you're denying any value at all that our lives may have—and that saps the spirit we need to soldier on. The hardest ordeal for us is the idea that we are causing grief for other people. We can put up with our own hardships okay, but the thought that our lives are the source of other people's unhappiness, that's plain unbearable.

Q24 *Would you like to be "normal"?*

What would we do if there was some way that we could be "normal"? Well, I bet the people around us—our parents and teachers—would be ecstatic with joy and say, "Hallelujah! We'll change them back to normal right now!" And for ages and ages I badly wanted to be normal, too. Living with special needs is so depressing and so relentless; I used to think it'd be the best thing if I could just live my life like a normal person.

But now, even if somebody developed a medicine to cure autism, I might well choose to stay as I am. Why have I come around to thinking this way?

To give the short version, I've learned that every human being, with or without disabilities, needs to strive to do their best, and by striving for happiness you will arrive at happiness. For us, you see, having autism is normal—so we can't know for sure what your "normal" is even like. But so long as we can learn to love ourselves, I'm not sure how much it matters whether we're normal or autistic.

Earthling and Autisman

I was traveling with my family to Hokkaido by airplane. It was the first time I'd flown for many years, and I was surprised to find that the sensation of gravity pulling at my body was really pleasant. I hadn't noticed this the time I'd flown before, because I was still a little kid back then. Anyway, I made up this very short story . . .

Once upon a time on a small, green, quiet planet.

Autisman: So—welcome to my home world.
Earthling: Don't you feel weighed down? It feels as if I've got weights strapped to my arms and legs.
Autisman: Ah, but on your planet, *I* always feel as if I'm swimming around in space, weightlessly.
Earthling: Okay. Now I understand you. I really understand.

If only there was a planet somewhere with a gravitational pull perfect for people with autism, then we'd be able to move around freely.

Q25 *What's the reason you jump?*

What do you think I'm feeling when I'm jumping up and
down clapping my hands? I bet you think I'm not really
feeling anything much beyond the manic glee all over my
face.

But when I'm jumping, it's as if my feelings are going
upward to the sky. Really, my urge to be swallowed up by
the sky is enough to make my heart quiver. When I'm
jumping, I can feel my body parts really well, too—my
bounding legs and my clapping hands—and that makes me
feel so, so good.

So that's one reason why I jump, and recently I've noticed another reason. People with autism react physically
to feelings of happiness and sadness. So when something
happens that affects me emotionally, my body seizes up as
if struck by lightning.

"Seizing up" doesn't mean that my muscles literally get
stiff and immobile—rather, it means that I'm not free to
move the way I want. So by jumping up and down, it's as if

I'm shaking loose the ropes that are tying up my body. When I jump, I feel lighter, and I think the reason my body is drawn skyward is that the motion makes me want to change into a bird and fly off to some faraway place.

But constrained both by ourselves and by the people around us, all we can do is tweet-tweet, flap our wings and hop around in a cage. Ah, if only I could just flap my wings and soar away, into the big blue yonder, over the hills and far away!

Q26 *Why do you write letters in the air?*

People with autism often write letters in the air. *Are you trying to tell us something?* or *Are you thinking about something?* you must be wondering, I guess. In my case, I'm writing to confirm what I want to remember. As I write, I'm recalling what I've seen—not as scenes, but as letters, signs and symbols. Letters, symbols and signs are my closest allies because they never change. They just stay as they are, fixed in my memory. And whenever we're lonely or happy, in the same way that you might half hum a song to yourself, we summon up our letters. When I'm writing them out, I can forget everything else. I'm not alone when I'm with letters. Letters and symbols are much easier for us to grasp than spoken words, and we can be with them whenever we want.

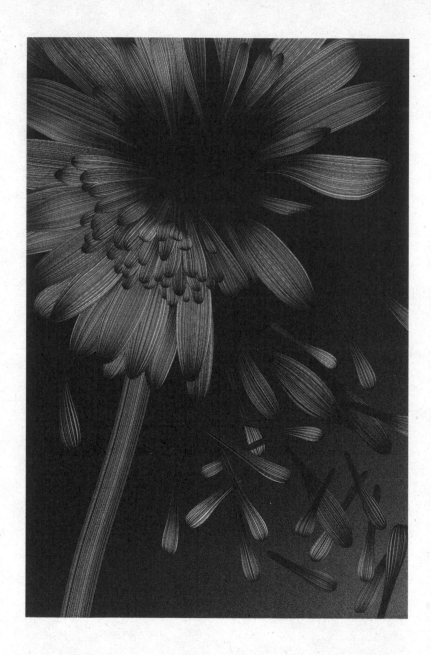

Q27 *Why do people with autism often cup their ears? Is it when there's a lot of noise?*

There are certain noises you don't notice but that really get to us. The problem here is that you don't understand how these noises affect us. It's not quite that the noises grate on our nerves. It's more to do with a fear that if we keep listening, we'll lose all sense of where we are. At times like these, it feels as if the ground is shaking and the landscape around us starts coming to get us, and it's absolutely terrifying. So cupping our ears is a measure we take to protect ourselves and get back our grip on where we are.

The noises that get to people with autism vary from person to person. I don't know how we'd cope if we couldn't cup our ears. Me too, I cup my ears sometimes, though I've gradually gotten used to the noises by pressing my hands over my ears less and less heavily. Some people can overcome the problem by slowly becoming accustomed to the noises, I guess. What matters most is that we learn to feel safe and secure even when the noises strike us.

Q28 *Why do you move your arms and legs about in that awkward way?*

In my gym class, the teacher tells me to do things like "Stretch your arms!" and "Bend at the knees!" But I don't always know what my arms and legs are up to, not exactly. For me, I have no clear sensation of where my arms and legs are attached, or how to make them do what I'm telling them to do. It's as if my limbs are a mermaid's rubbery tail.

I think the reason why some kids with autism try to get hold of an object by "borrowing" someone else's hand is that they can't tell how far they need to extend their own arms to reach the object. They're not too sure how to actually grab the object either, because we have problems perceiving and gauging distances. By constant practice, however, we should be able to overcome this difficulty.

That said, I still can't even tell when I've stepped on someone's foot or jostled someone out of my way. So something connected with my sense of touch might be miswired too.

Q29 *Why do you do things the rest of us don't? Do your senses work differently in some way?*

"Why won't you wear shoes?" "Why will you only wear half-length sleeves?" "Why do you always shave off or pluck out your body hair? Doesn't it hurt?" Every time us people with autism do something that other people wouldn't, it must make you wonder why. Do people with autism possess different senses? Or do these actions just give us some sort of kick?

To my mind, both answers are barking up the wrong tree. The reason could be that we've gotten into such a state that if we *don't* do these actions, we'll go to pieces completely. If you talk about someone's "senses working differently," it means that the person's nervous system is somehow malfunctioning. But I believe that in our case, there's nothing wrong with us at a nerve level. Instead, it's actually our emotions that trigger the abnormal reactions. It's only natural for anyone stuck in a bad place to try to get out of it, and it's my own despair that causes me to misread the messages my senses are sending me. If all of my attention gets focused on one area of my body, it's as if all of my body's energy is concentrated there too, which is when my senses all report that something in that area is going badly wrong.

If a person without autism is going through a hard time, he or she can talk it over with someone, or make a ruckus about it. But in our case, that's not an option—we can never make ourselves understood. Even when we're in the middle of a panic attack, people either don't get what's happening to us, or else they just tell us to stop crying. My guess is that the despair we're feeling has nowhere to go and fills up our entire bodies, making our senses more and more confused.

Q30 Why are you too sensitive or insensitive to pain?

Among people with autism, there are some who make a huge fuss when they have their hair or nails trimmed, even though it shouldn't hurt at all. At the same time, there are people who stay very calm and collected even when they've got an injury that's obviously painful.

I don't think this is all to do with nerves and nerve endings. It's more a matter of "inner pain" expressing itself via the body. When memories suddenly come to people, we experience a flashback—but in the case of people with autism, memories are not stored in a clear order. For those of us who are disturbed by having their hair and nails trimmed, somehow their negative memories are probably connected to the action.

A normal person might say, "Oh, he's never liked having his hair cut or his nails trimmed, ever since he was small, and we've no idea why." But the thing is, the memory of a person with autism isn't like a number-scale from which you pick out the recollection you're after: it's more like a jigsaw puzzle, where if even just one piece is misinserted, the entire puzzle becomes impossible to complete. What's more, a single piece that doesn't belong there can mess up all the surrounding memories as well. So it's not necessarily physical pain that's making us cry at all—quite possibly, it's memory.

As for people who don't show any signs of pain, my guess is that they're unable to keep those signs on display. I think it's very difficult for you to properly get your heads around just how hard it is for us to express what we're feeling. For us, dealing with the pain by treating it as if it's already gone is actually easier than letting other people know we are in pain.

Normal people think we're highly dependent and can't live without ongoing support, but in fact there are times when we're stoic heroes.

Q31 *Why are you so picky about what you eat?*

Some people with autism keep to a very limited diet, it's true. I don't really have this problem myself, but to some degree I can understand where they're coming from, I think. We do this business called eating three times a day, but for some people having to eat different meals each time can be a major headache. Each type of food has its distinct taste, color and shape. Usually, these differences are what make eating a pleasure, but for some people with autism, only those foodstuffs they can already think of as food have any taste. Everything else is about as appetizing as toy food you might be served at a little kid's "pretend tea-time."

So why do these people experience new food this way? You could say, "Because their sense of taste is all messed up" and be done with it. But couldn't you also say that they just need more time than the average person to come to appreciate unknown types of food? Even if they'd be happy sticking with only those foods they're used to eating, in my opinion meals aren't just about nutrition—meals are also about finding joy in life. Eating is living, and picky eaters should definitely be nudged toward trying different foods little by little. That's what I reckon, anyway.

Q32 *When you look at something, what do you see first?*

So how do people with autism see the world, exactly? We, and only we, can ever know the answer to that one! Sometimes I actually pity you for not being able to see the beauty of the world in the same way we do. Really, our vision of the world can be incredible, just incredible . . .

You might reply, "But the eyes we all use to look at things work the same way, right?" Fair enough, you may be looking at the exact same things as us, but *how* we perceive them appears to be different. When you see an object, it seems that you see it as an entire thing first, and only afterward do its details follow on. But for people with autism, the details jump straight out at us first of all, and then only gradually, detail by detail, does the whole image sort of float up into focus. What part of the whole image captures our eyes first depends on a number of things. When a color is vivid or a shape is eye-catching, then that's the detail that claims our attention, and then our hearts kind of drown in it, and we can't concentrate on anything else.

Every single thing has its own unique beauty. People with autism get to cherish this beauty, as if it's a kind of blessing given to us. Wherever we go, whatever we do, we can never be completely lonely. We may look like we're not with anyone, but we're always in the company of friends.

Q33 *Is it difficult for you to choose appropriate clothing?*

Whether it's hot or whether it's cold, I always have a hard time choosing the right clothing, as well as putting extra layers on or peeling them off accordingly. Some people with autism keep wearing exactly the same type of clothes all through the year, in fact. What's the deal here? What's so tricky about putting on or taking off clothes as you need to?

Well—search me. It might be scorching hot, and we *know* it's scorching hot, but it simply might not occur to a person with autism that taking off a layer is a good idea. It's not that we don't understand the logic—it's just that we somehow forget. We forget what we're wearing, and how to make ourselves cooler.

I can mop the sweat off my face with my handkerchief, at least—I'm used to doing this now—but adjusting my clothing is a taller order because the situation is often changing. So I can well sympathize with those people with autism who prefer to wear the same clothes day in, day out.

Clothes are like an extension of our bodies, an outer skin, and so the day-in, day-outers find it reassuring to stick to the same outfit. We feel obliged to do everything we can to protect ourselves against uncertainty, and wearing comfy clothes we like is one way of doing this.

Q34 *Do you have a sense of time?*

Time is a continuous thing with no clear boundaries, which is why it's so confusing for people with autism. Perhaps you're puzzled about why time intervals and the speed of time are so hard for us to gauge, and why time seems such slippery stuff for people with autism.

For us, time is as difficult to grasp as picturing a country we've never been to. You can't capture the passing of time on a piece of paper. The hands of a clock may show that some time has passed, but the fact that we can't actually *feel* it makes us nervous.

Because I have autism, I know all about this and I feel it myself—believe me, this is scary stuff. We're anxious about what kind of condition we'll be in at a future point, and what problems we'll trigger. People who have effortless control over themselves and their bodies never really experience this fear.

For us, one second is infinitely long—yet twenty-four hours can hurtle by in a flash. Time can only be fixed in our memories in the form of visual scenes. For this reason there's not a lot of difference between one second and twenty-four hours. Exactly what the next moment has in store for us never stops being a big, big worry.

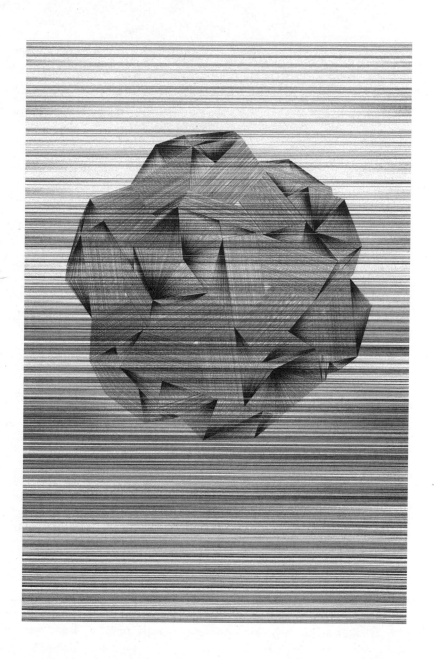

Q35 *Why are your sleep patterns all messed up?*

Quite a few people with autism find it hard to fall asleep at night. When I was little there were times when I couldn't fall asleep either, even when it got really late. This seems strange, because we human beings aren't nocturnal animals, right? But now I rarely have this problem. The cure might simply be time. People who can't sleep may appear to be okay on the outside, while inside they're exhausted.

I don't really know what causes sleeping disorders, so all I want to ask you to do here is, if your autistic child isn't going to sleep at a decent hour, please don't tell them off—even if it goes on night after night after night.

Never-ending Summer

People with autism can be restless and fidgety all the time, almost to the point of it looking comical. It's as if it's summer for us the whole year round. Most people look pretty relaxed when they're not doing anything in particular, but we're always zooming off madly like a kid who's late for school. We're like cicadas who'll miss the summer unless we hurry, hurry, hurry. *Bzzzzzz, bzzzzzz, crick-crick, crick-crick, chirrrrrr . . .* We cry our hearts out, shout our heads off, and never rest in our battle against time.

As autumn comes around the year's corner, the cicadas' lives come to an end. Human beings still have plenty of time in store, but we who have autism, who are semi-detached from the flow of time, we are always uneasy from sunrise to sunset. Just like the cicadas, we cry out, we call out.

Q36 *Why do you like spinning?*

Us people with autism often enjoy spinning ourselves around and around. We like spinning whatever object comes to hand, for that matter. Can you understand what's so much fun about spinning?

Everyday scenery doesn't rotate, so things that do spin simply fascinate us. Just watching spinning things fills us with a sort of everlasting bliss—for the time we sit watching them, they rotate with perfect regularity. Whatever object we spin, this is always true. Unchanging things are comforting, and there's something beautiful about that.

Q37 *Why do you flap your fingers and hands in front of your face?*

Flapping our fingers and hands in front of our faces allows the light to enter our eyes in a pleasant, filtered fashion. Light that reaches us like this feels soft and gentle, like moonlight. But "unfiltered" direct light sort of "needles" its way into the eyeballs of people with autism in sharp straight lines, so we see too many points of light. This actually makes our eyes hurt.

This said, we couldn't get by without light. Light wipes away our tears, and when we're bathed in light, we're happy. Perhaps we just love how its particles pour down on us. Light particles somehow console us. I admit this is something I can't quite explain using logic.

Q38 *Why do you line up your toy cars and blocks?*

Lining things up is the best fun. Watching running water is great fun, too. Other kids seem to enjoy games about pretending and make-believe, but as a person with autism I never really see the point of them.

What I care about—in fact I'm pretty obsessive about this—is the order things come in, and different ways of lining them up. It's actually the lines and the surfaces of things like jigsaw puzzles that we love, and things like that. When we're playing in this way, our brains feel refreshed and clear.

Q39 *Why do you like being in the water?*

We just want to go back. To the distant, distant past. To a primeval era, in fact, before human beings even existed. All people with autism feel the same about this one, I reckon. Aquatic life-forms came into being and evolved, but why did they then have to emerge onto dry land, and turn into human beings who chose to lead lives ruled by time? These are real mysteries to me.

In the water it's so quiet and I'm so free and happy there. Nobody hassles us in the water, and it's as if we've got all the time in the world. Whether we stay in one place or whether we're swimming about, when we're in the water we can really be at one with the pulse of time. Outside of the water there's always too much stimulation for our eyes and our ears, and it's impossible for us to guess how long one second is or how long an hour takes.

People with autism have no freedom. The reason is that we are a different kind of human, born with primeval senses. We are outside the normal flow of time, we can't express ourselves, and our bodies are hurtling us through life. If only we could go back to that distant, distant, watery past—then we'd all be able to live as contentedly and as freely as you lot!

This is a difficult one. I'm not quite sure what the answer is. If you figured that we must like TV commercials just because the slogans and catchphrases roll off our tongues so easily, that wouldn't be the full story. We remember them as well as we do because they're on so often, and sure, we dash to the TV when a familiar commercial comes on. We enjoy watching the ones we know well. How come you people without autism aren't that keen on TV commercials? They're on again and again and again, after all—so isn't seeing them a bit like being visited by old and dear friends?

I'm not a big fan of TV commercials in and of themselves, but when a familiar ad comes on, I get quite excited about it. This is because when a familiar one comes on I already know what it's talking about, and I feel sort of soothed knowing that they never last for long. The reason why we look happy to your eyes while we're watching TV ads must be that at all other times we're less stable and calm, and our faces are blanker. Perhaps what you're getting when you look at us watching commercials on the TV is a brief glimpse of the Real Us.

Q41 *What kind of TV programs do you enjoy?*

Even at my age, I still enjoy this TV program for kinder-garten kids, *Watching with Mother*. Reading that, you must be thinking, "Ah, this guy's just a big kid, after all!" But that's not the case, in my humble opinion. Sure, we may appear to resemble small children—our fondness for gen-tle, kind, beautiful things—but we tend to prefer simpler, more straightforward stories, not because of childishness, but because we can more easily guess what's going to hap-pen next. This allows us to stay more relaxed and more engaged. Plus the simpler stories tend to repeat themselves a lot, so when we get to a familiar scene we can get all ex-cited and make a happy fuss.

People with autism get quite a kick out of repetition. If I was asked how come, my reply would be this: "When you're in a strange new place, aren't *you* relieved too if you run into a friendly, familiar face?"

What we just don't do are disputes, bargaining or criti-cizing others. We're totally helpless in these scenarios.

A Story I Heard Somewhere

———————

There was once a girl who loved dancing and she wore red shoes. Everybody who knew her thought, *That girl will keep dancing until the day she dies,* and who knows, maybe the girl thought the same thing herself.

One night, when the whole world was fast asleep, she began dancing. She went:

A twirl and a whirl and a leaping curl,
A-skippetty-skippetty skip-skip-skip,
A-tappetty-tappetty tap-tap-tap,
A-tra-lah-di-dah and a tim tam tom.

The girl was in a state of sheer bliss. *How sublime it is to dance!* A whole week went by in this manner. Then she thought, *I wonder how much longer I can keep this up?* By this point she was almost dead on her feet, but all she wished for was to keep on dancing, dancing, dancing.

Then, on the eighth day, this handsome young man

appeared. He said to her, "Would you care to dance with me?" With that, the girl stopped dancing. She said, "Thanks, but no. I've just discovered something more precious than dancing." Then, in a small house, they lived happily ever after.

Because it's fun! We get a real kick out of numbers, us people with autism. Numbers are fixed, unchanging things. The number 1, for example, is only ever, ever the number 1. That simplicity, that clearness, it's so comforting to us.

Whoever reads any given timetable or calendar, it's always, always the same. You can easily understand all of them by following the same set of rules. And when it comes to our favorite things, we can memorize these as easily as if they were jumping straight into our heads. Invisible things like human relationships and ambiguous expressions, however, these are difficult for us people with autism to get our heads around.

Perhaps you're thinking that it's no major effort for me to write these sentences, but that wouldn't be true at all. Always lurking at the back of my mind is an anxiety about whether or not I'm perceiving things in the same way that people without autism do. So, via TV, books and just tuning in to the people around me, I'm constantly learning about how ordinary people are supposed to feel in given situations. And whenever I learn something new, I write a short story dealing with the situation in question. This way, with luck, it won't slip my mind.

No, I don't dislike longer sentences. Whatever else is going on, I'm always hungry to learn about lots of different things. It really gets me down that people just don't understand how hungry for knowledge people with autism actually are. The problem isn't that I dislike longer sentences. The problem is that my patience wears out so quickly. I get tired so soon and lose all track of what the sentence was about. I can read simple picture books without much trouble, so when I'm alone, I tend to choose one of these. They are easy to follow and stimulate my imagination, and I never get bored with them.

I want to grow up learning a million things! There must be countless other people with autism who have the same desire, the same attitude. But our problem is, we aren't capable of studying all by ourselves. To be able to study like other people, we need more time and different strategies and approaches. And those people who help us study, they actually need more patience than we do. They need to understand our eagerness to learn, even though from the outside we may not appear to be keen students. But we are. We, too, want to grow.

Q44 *What do you think about running races?*

I don't hate races, but the instant I'm conscious of the need to run fast, I find that I can't. If I'm just running for fun with my friends, I find I can run as long as I want to—it's as if I'm making friends with the wind. Sometimes people say that I'm very good at running away, but really it's just that when someone's chasing me, I find it both funny and frightening when the chaser is catching up to me. This prompts me to put on a spurt of speed, and I'm off.

The reason I can't run well once I'm aware of needing to isn't to do with nerves. My problem is that as soon as I try to run fast, I start thinking about how I ought to be moving my arms and legs, and then my whole body freezes up. And another reason I don't do well in races is that I don't really get any pleasure out of beating other people. I agree that it's right and proper to do the best you can in a race, but this desire to beat everyone else is another matter altogether. So on competitive occasions like school sports days, the pleasure I get just by being there takes over, and I'll end up running the race with all the urgency of someone skipping his way across a meadow.

Q45 *Why do you enjoy going out for walks so much?*

My guess is that lots of people with autism like walking, and I wonder if you can work out why. "Because walking makes you feel good?" "Because it's great being out in the open air?" Both these replies are true, of course, but for me the number one reason is that us people with autism love the greenness of nature. Now you might be thinking, "Oh, is that all?" However, our fondness for nature is, I think, a little bit different from everyone else's. I'm guessing that what touches you in nature is the beauty of the trees and the flowers and things. But to us people with special needs, nature is as important as our own lives. The reason is that when we look at nature, we receive a sort of permission to be alive in this world, and our entire bodies get recharged. However often we're ignored and pushed away by other people, nature will always give us a good big hug, here inside our hearts.

The greenness of nature is the lives of plants and trees. Green is life. And that's the reason we love to go out for walks.

Q46 *Do you enjoy your free time?*

So what do *you* do in your free time? Because for people with autism, free time is in fact un-free time. "You can do whatever you feel like doing now," someone might tell us. But actually, it's pretty hard for us to find something we do feel like doing, not just like that. If we happen to see some toys or books we're always playing with or reading, then sure, we'll pick them up. Thing is, however, that's not so much what we *want* to do as something we *can* do. Playing with familiar items is comforting because we already know what to do with them, so then, of course, people watching us assume, *Aha, so that's what he likes to do in his free time* . . . What I really want to do, however, is to get stuck in some difficult book or to debate some issue or other.

We are misunderstood, and we'd give anything if only we could be understood properly. People with autism would be suffering breakdowns over this—all the time— if we weren't holding ourselves in so tightly. Please, understand what we really are, and what we're going through.

Q47 *Would you give us an example of something people with autism really enjoy?*

We do take pleasure in one thing that you probably won't be able to guess. Namely, making friends with nature. The reason we aren't much good at people skills is that we think too much about what sort of impression we're making on the other person, or how we should be responding to this or that. But nature is always there at hand to wrap us up, gently: glowing, swaying, bubbling, rustling.

Just by looking at nature, I feel as if I'm being swallowed up into it, and in that moment I get the sensation that my body's now a speck, a speck from long before I was born, a speck that is melting into nature herself. This sensation is so amazing that I forget that I'm a human being, and one with special needs to boot.

Nature calms me down when I'm furious, and laughs with me when I'm happy. You might think that it's not possible that nature could be a friend, not really. But human beings are part of the animal kingdom too, and perhaps us people with autism still have some leftover awareness of this, buried somewhere deep down. I'll always cherish the part of me that thinks of nature as a friend.

The Great Statue
of Buddha

———

When you've been on a trip somewhere, have you ever watched someone burst into tears for no obvious reason? Of course there *is* a reason for it, really, it's just that the person who's crying isn't able to tell you what the reason is. For all you know, the person might be crying for joy, but that might not even occur to you.

Well, it's much the same for me. The other day I was visiting a town called Kamakura, where there's this huge statue of Buddha. And when I saw it, I was so deeply moved that I started welling up. It wasn't just Buddha's majesty and dignity, it was the sheer weight of history and generations of people's hopes, prayers and thoughts that broke over me, and I couldn't stop myself crying. It was as if Buddha himself was saying to me, "All human beings have their hardships to bear, so never swerve away from the path you're on."

Everybody has a heart that can be touched by something. Crying isn't necessarily about sadness or meltdowns or being upset. I'd like you to bear that in mind, if you would.

Q48 *Why are you always running off somewhere?*

My mind is forever swaying, this way and that. It's not that I want to go running off, I just can't help dashing away to whatever place enters my line of sight. It's really annoying for me too, because people are always telling me off about it. But I don't know how to stop it.

So I'm not doing all this moving around because it pleases me—it isn't even all that calming. It's like being teleported from one place to another without knowing it's happening. Even if someone tries to prevent me, or if something else gets in the way, it happens anyway. I sort of lose myself for a little while.

So what's my master plan to fix this problem? I'm constantly battling this impulse to run off and, compared to how it used to be, I'm slowly getting better at controlling it, I think. But I haven't found a really effective way to fix this problem yet. Jogging and walking refresh my body, at least, and once refreshed, I kind of feel back home inside myself. My sense of gravity is restored, too, and that calms me down.

Q49 *Why do you get lost so often?*

I've already mentioned how I dash off as soon as I spot anything interesting. There's a different reason for why we get lost so often, however, and I think it's this: we don't really know where we ought to be. You could tell us that we ought to follow someone else, or hold their hand, but the fact is that, with or without your suggestion, we're still going to lose our way.

Simply put, people with autism never, ever feel at ease, wherever we are. Because of this, we wander off— or run away—in search of some location where we *do* feel at ease. While we're on this search, it doesn't occur to us to consider how or where we're going to end up. We get swallowed up by the illusion that unless we can find a place to belong, we are going to be all alone in the world. Then eventually we get lost, and have to be escorted back to the place we were at, or the person we were with, before.

But our uneasy, unsettled feeling doesn't go away. I don't think we'll ever be able to reach our Shangri-La, however. I know it exists only in the depths of the forest or at the bottom of the deep blue sea.

Q50 *Why do you wander off from home?*

Once, when I was a little kid at kindergarten, I wandered off from home and had to be picked up by the police. Back then, in fact, I used to leave home quite regularly and, as I look back from this distance, I can think of several reasons why I did it. It wasn't because I wanted to go out for a specific purpose, like wanting fresh air. It was because—this is hard to put into words—my body moved because it was lured outside by something there.

As I was walking farther from home, I didn't feel any fear or anxiety. It came down to this: if I didn't go outside, then I would cease to exist. Why? I can't say, but I *had* to keep walking, on and on and on. Turning back was not permitted, because roads never come to an end. Roads speak to us people with autism, and invite us onward. There's not much logic in any of this, I know. Until someone brings us back home, we don't know what we've done, and then we're as shocked as anyone.

I stopped wandering off from home on the day I very

nearly got mowed down by a car, because the fear of it made a deep impact on my memory. So when something drastic enough happens, I think we can rein in this habit of wandering off. Meanwhile, please keep an eye out for us . . .

Q51 *Why do you repeat certain actions again and again?*

The reason people with autism repeat actions isn't simply because they enjoy what they're doing. Watching us, some people can get shocked, as if we were possessed. However much you like doing something, it would normally be impossible to keep doing it as often as we do, right? But the repetition doesn't come from our own free will. It's more like our brains keep sending out the same order, time and time again. Then, while we're repeating the action, we get to feel really good and incredibly comforted.

From our standpoint, I feel a deep envy of people who can know what their own minds are saying, and who have the power to act accordingly. My brain is always sending me off on little missions, whether or not I want to do them. And if I don't obey, then I have to fight a feeling of horror. Really, it's like I'm being pushed over the brink into a kind of Hell.

For people with autism, living itself is a battle.

Q52 *Why don't you do what you're supposed to do,*
even after being told a million times?

Kids with autism do what we're not supposed to do again
and again, however many times you've told us not to. We
understand what you're telling us okay, but somehow we
just repeat the sequence. This happens to me, too, and
I've thought about how the sequence gets imprinted. First
I do some action or other that I'm not allowed to; then
something else happens as a result; and then I get told
off for it; and last, my impulse to re-create this sequence
trumps the knowledge that I've been told not to do it, and
I end up doing it again. The next thing I know, I feel a sort
of electrical buzz in my brain, which is very pleasant—no
other sensation is quite the same. Perhaps the closest thing
is watching your very favorite scene on a DVD, looping on
auto-repeat, over and over.

Still, we shouldn't do what we shouldn't do. How, as
thinking beings, can we break out of this loop? This is a big
project. I work hard to solve the problem, but this work

costs so much energy. Maintaining this grip on myself is really, really, really tough. It's at these times that we need your help with patience, guidance and love. Of course we want you to stop us from doing what we're not supposed to do, but we also want you to understand what we're going through at these times.

We don't obsess over certain things because we like it, or because we want to. People with autism obsess over certain things because we'd go crazy if we didn't. By performing whatever action it is, we feel a bit soothed and calmed down. But then whenever someone tells me off for doing the action, or even prevents me from repeating it, I feel utterly miserable. I never actually wanted to do it in the first place, and now I end up hating myself even more for not being able to control my own actions. Whenever our obsessive behavior is bothering other people, please stop us right away, whatever way you can. The person who's suffering the most is the one who's causing all the headaches for everyone else—that is, the one with the autism. Even though it looks as if we're frolicking about and having the best time, inside we're aching and hurting because we know we don't even have control over what our own bodies are doing.

All that said, when our obsessive behavior isn't actually

bothering anyone, I'd ask you just to keep a quiet eye on us. It won't last forever. One fine day, however hard we have tried to will ourselves to stop before, the obsessive action suddenly stops itself, without warning—like, "How come?" Somehow our brain flashes up a GAME OVER signal. The sign works like when you've just guzzled down an entire bag of sweets. The need to obsess about whatever it was is all used up. When that sign appears, I feel set free, like someone who can finally put aside all of last night's dreams.

The problem is, how to help people with autism stop their obsessive actions in cases when they *are* bothering others? To you who are helping us, I'd say this: please handle and approach our behavioral issues with a strong faith that they are definitely going to pass, at some point in the future. When we are stopped from doing what we want, we may well make a terrible song and dance about it, but in time we'll get used to the idea. And until we reach that point, we'd like you to stick with it, and stick with us.

The Black Crow and the White Dove

———

There was once a black crow who liked a certain song called "The Seven Little Crows," which began, *Crow, Crow, Crow, why do you caw?* Except in this song, crows in stories are bullies and villains who everyone hates. This troubled the black crow, who would ask himself, *How come it's always the crows who are the bad guys?*

One day, a white dove who had lost her way met the black crow. She asked, "Where does this path go?" Then the white dove stared down at the ground, looking lonely.

The black crow wondered what was wrong, and asked, "What's the matter?"

On the point of tears, the white dove said, "I've been searching for the path to happiness for a long, long time, but I still can't find it anywhere. And I'm supposed to be the bird of peace, too . . ."

The black crow was surprised to learn that even a bird as beautiful and as loved by everyone as the white dove nonetheless had deep problems to worry about. His answer was this: "But all paths are one connected path."

The white dove looked taken aback by this unexpected answer. But after a time, she smiled. "How about that? So the path I've been searching for all this time is the path I am already on." In excellent spirits, the white dove flew off, up into the blue sky. Then the black crow, too, turned his head skyward, then flapped his wings vigorously, and away he flew. And the black crow looked no less perfect against the deep blue than the white dove.

Q54 *Why do you need cues and prompts?*

People with autism are sometimes unable to move on to their next action without a verbal prompt. For example, even after we ask for a glass of juice and are given it, we won't actually start drinking until someone's said, "Enjoy" or "Go ahead and drink, then." Or even after the person with autism has announced, "Right, I'll hang the laundry now," he won't get started until someone has said back, "Okay, that's great."

I don't really know why some people with autism need these cues, but I do know that I'm one of them. Since we already know what we'll be doing next, surely we should just be able to get on with it unprompted, right? Yes, I think so too! But the fact is, doing the action without the cue can be really, really tough. In the same way as you don't walk across the street until the light turns green, I can't "switch on" the next action until my brain receives the right prompt. Doing the next action without obeying "the prompt rule" is terrifying. It's enough to make me lose the plot completely.

Once we're through the terrifying phase, we can, bit by bit, become used to the idea that doing things without the prompt is possible. But getting to that point isn't something we can do alone—as you can tell, by the mega-fuss we make every time. We cry, we scream, we hit out and break things. But still, we *don't* want you to give up on us. Please, keep battling alongside us. We are the ones who are suffering the most in these scenes, and badly, badly want to free ourselves from our own chains.

Q55 *Why can you never stay still?*

My body's always moving about. I just can't stay still. When I'm not moving, it feels as if my soul is detaching itself from my body, and this makes me so jumpy and scared that I can't stay where I am. I'm always on the lookout for an exit. But even though I'm forever wanting to be someplace else, I can never actually find my way there. I'm always struggling inside my own body, and staying still really hammers it home that I'm trapped here. But as long as I'm in a state of motion, I'm able to relax a little bit.

Everyone tells people with autism, "Calm down, stop fidgeting, stay still," when we're busy moving around. But because I feel so much more relaxed when I *am* moving, it took me quite a while to work out exactly what their "calm down" even meant. Finally, I've come to understand that there are times when I'm not supposed to be moving about. The only way we can learn to do this is by practicing, a little at a time.

I understand that any plan is only a plan, and is never definite, but I just cannot take it when a fixed arrangement doesn't proceed as per the visual schedule. I understand that changes can't always be avoided, but my brain shouts back, *No way, that's not acceptable*. So speaking for myself, I'm not a big fan of having visual schedules around the place. People with autism may look happier with pictures and diagrams of where we're supposed to be and when, but in fact we end up being restricted by them. They make us feel like robots, with each and every action preprogrammed. What I'd suggest is that instead of showing us visual schedules, you talk through the day's plan with us, verbally and beforehand. Visual schedules create such a strong impression on us that if a change occurs, we get flustered and panicky.

Observing that the new change can also be shown on the schedule is beside the point, I'm afraid. The message I want to get across here is: please don't use visual things like pictures on our schedules, because then the activities on the schedules, and their times and timings, get imprinted too vividly onto our memories. And when that happens, we end up stressing ourselves over whether what we're doing now is or isn't matching up with what was on the schedule. In my case, I end up checking the time so often that I'm no longer able to enjoy what I'm doing.

People who don't live with autism often think that the rest of us won't be able to understand the plan for the day just by listening. But give it a try, and although we might ask you the same questions over and over, we will get the hang of it, and ask you less and less. Sure, this will take time, but I think it's easier for us in the long run. Of course, when it comes to explaining the order that you do certain actions in, or instructions about how to make such-and-such an object, visual aids, like pictures, can help us a lot. But being shown photos of places we're going to visit on an upcoming school trip, for example, can spoil our fun.

Q57 *What causes panic attacks and meltdowns?*

I don't know if you can understand this one. Panic attacks can be triggered by many things, but even if you set up an ideal environment that gets rid of all the usual causes for a given person, we would *still* suffer panic attacks now and then.

One of the biggest misunderstandings you have about us is your belief that our feelings aren't as subtle and complex as yours. Because how we behave can appear so childish in your eyes, you tend to assume that we're childish on the inside, too. But of course, we experience the same emotions that you do. And because people with autism aren't skillful talkers, we may in fact be even more sensitive than you are. Stuck here inside these unresponsive bodies of ours, with feelings we can't properly express, it's always a struggle just to survive. And it's this feeling of helplessness that sometimes drives us half crazy, and brings on a panic attack or a meltdown.

When this is happening to us, please just let us cry, or yell, and get it all out. Stay close by and keep a gentle eye on us, and while we're swept up in our torment, please stop us from hurting ourselves or others.

Q58 *What are your thoughts on autism itself?*

I think that people with autism are born outside the regime of civilization. Sure, this is just my own made-up theory, but I think that, as a result of all the killings in the world and the selfish planet-wrecking that humanity has committed, a deep sense of crisis exists.

Autism has somehow arisen out of this. Although people with autism look like other people physically, we are in fact very different in many ways. We are more like travelers from the distant, distant past. And if, by our being here, we could help the people of the world remember what truly matters for the Earth, that would give us a quiet pleasure.

 wrote this story in the hope that it will help you to understand how painful it is when you can't express yourself to the people you love. If this story connects with your heart in some way, then I believe you'll be able to connect back to the hearts of people with autism too.

I'm Right Here

Shun used to think that he knew himself very well, but from that day on he was no longer sure. *Everyone's staring at my face.* The early evening sky was ominous with orange clouds bound by ash-grey. *Why are they all staring at me?* When Shun had emerged from his local supermarket, an old man came over and asked, "What are you doing here?" Shun had never met him before. He wore a red hat pulled down low over his eyes, a white T-shirt and black knee-length shorts, even though it was winter. *Never talk to strangers,* Shun had told himself, and started hurrying for home. And that was the moment when Shun noticed— *everyone's staring at my face.* His first thought was that everyone was worrying about him, but no, it wasn't that kind of look . . . How to put it? Not a surprised look, not a searching gaze . . . more of an icy, heart-chilling stare. Whatever it was, Shun ran off home.

"I'm back!"

Shun was relieved to get back home, safe and sound at

last. His mom was busy preparing supper as usual. Shun opened the fridge and spoke to his mom while he took out a carton of juice. "Hey, Mom, today I . . ." Then Shun's words just dried up. She was just standing there. Apron on, pan in hand, her hair and clothes the same as they were when Shun had left home earlier, but still, Shun couldn't move a muscle. *That icy stare again.* Everything seemed to be revolving around him in slow motion. *Get away from here, go, now, get out!* Was Shun thinking this, or was someone ordering him? Shun managed to marshal his unmoving body into action, and he fled outside, almost howling.

Shun found himself in a park, with no memory of how he'd arrived there. Even though it was cold, his body was soaked in sweat. He was exhausted. *What's going on?* To try to get a grip on things, Shun decided to look back over the day. *I woke up, I went to school, I came home. So far, so normal. And after that . . . after that . . .* He remembered nothing. *What the hell did I do next?* Shun sat on his bench, staring into space, while the wintry wind blew all around him. Like the hole in the middle of a doughnut, the memory had somehow fallen out from Shun's mind. He couldn't even cry. *How strange that a person can keep his head, even when things have become as desperate as this.* The sun was sinking low now. *I have to do something about this,* Shun thought, yet at the same time, he was also feeling, *Whatever happens to me, happens.* How much time had gone by? Shun noticed darkness all around him. He hauled himself to his feet.

With no clear destination in mind, Shun carried on walking. Nobody else was around. Maybe all the people were in their houses. However lonely Shun might have felt, he didn't want to see anyone, not even his friends. *I wonder if they're worrying about me at home by now?* Shun's feet led him back to his house.

But it looked as though his house was in complete darkness. Shun's dad was supposed to come home from work early that day, so Shun wondered where his parents could have gone. At the same time, he felt relief to be back. *They must have gone out to look for me,* he thought. *And it wasn't as if anyone was actually hassling me earlier, they kept staring at me in that weird way, that's all.* Feeling much better now, Shun decided to wait for his parents in front of his house. The winter sky at night was beautiful, and the flickering of the stars soothed his heart.

Footsteps drew nearer. *That must be Mom and Dad.*

Shun went running up to them. "I'm really, really sorry to make you worry about me, I just . . ." But something was very wrong about them. *Maybe they can't recognize me in the dark?* So Shun grabbed his mother by her arm . . .

. . . or he thought he did, but her arm wasn't there. *What? This can't be happening!* Shun had absolutely no idea what was going on. He just stood there, struck dumb, as his parents walked by, right in front of him. All Shun could do was repeat to himself, *This can't be true, it can't be true.* He crouched on the ground, hugging his knees. *What's happening to me? What's going on? Help me. Help . . .*

"Ah, so here you are." Shun heard a voice and looked up. Standing there was the old man he'd met outside the supermarket. He was looking down at Shun with a kind face. "You're all right. You're all right. Let's go back together." The old man took hold of Shun's hand.

Shun just looked at the old man.

Softly, the old man told Shun, "You don't belong to this world anymore."

Shun didn't have a clue what he was talking about.

"Shun," the old man said, "you didn't notice the moment that you died. On your way to the supermarket, I'm afraid you were hit by a car that ran the red light."

The memory of the scene slowly returned to Shun. *Yeah, that's right, I meant to dodge the car, but then I sort of froze and couldn't move, yes, then I was hit,* and I thought, What an ungodly mess *this* is going to be, *but then I came to again and there I was, still outside the supermarket . . .* Shun's eyes began to brim with tears. *So I'm dead? Me? Dead? And I can't even stop blubbering . . . I don't want to be dead. No. No, no. No!*

Shun cried, and he kept on crying.

How much time had gone by? Nobody can cry forever, after all. By and by Shun's tears dried up, but his mind was still blank. The old man spoke: "Righto. What say we go back now?"

Back? Go back where? "But my home's right . . . here." Shun had a quick peek into his house through the window. He could see into the living room. *Crying . . . Mom and Dad are both crying their eyes out.*

Shun's eyes started filling up once again.

So what am I supposed to do now?

The old man motioned to Shun and began walking, and, as if drawn after him by an invisible cord, Shun followed. The old man strode out toward the west. *What's waiting for me up ahead?* Even though Shun was dead, he was still gripped by the fear of death. In a quaking voice he asked, "Where are we going?"

The old man put his arm around Shun's shoulder and replied matter-of-factly: "We're off to Heaven, of course."

"Oh. I've, um . . . never been to Heaven before."

The old man laughed out loud. "Obviously."

The Path to Heaven. *Yes, I read about it in a book, a long time ago. . . . It was a beautiful white path leading upward to Heaven, with the loveliest never-ever-seen flowers all around.* Thinking these things, Shun kept pace with the old man. About half an hour may have passed. Shun was wondering if the Path to Heaven could really be as plain and dull as this one. What's more, he didn't feel the remotest bit dead. Even though things had looked so desperate and bleak before, Shun was now feeling much more like his old self again. "Excuse me, sir, will we be arriving in Heaven any time soon? It's just that I feel tired enough to keel over and die."

The old man snorted out a laugh.

So Shun snorted out a laugh, too.

Who would have guessed it? thought Shun. *You can*

find something to laugh at in any situation, even when you're dead. Mulling this over, Shun found he was feeling happier.

"Well, you finally smiled about something," said the old man. "Then the Path to Heaven begins right here." Serenely, he raised both his hands toward the sky. He seemed to be saying something, but Shun couldn't catch what it was.

Now that I think of it, somebody once told me how when we die, we become stars. Must have been Mom, I guess. She was always on my side. Dad gave me a lot of time too, mind . . . but no more games of tossing a ball to each other now . . . Shun looked up at the night sky and gave a small sigh.

"What d'you reckon?" said the old man. "Time to be off?"

Shun grew afraid again. *Am I dying? No, no, I'm already dead. But what's going to happen to me now? If only Mom . . .* Shun's whole body started shaking.

The old man noticed. He gave Shun a concerned hug. "There's nothing to worry about. You'll only be gone for an instant."

Only gone for an instant? Shun was confused. *What's going to become of me?* Slowly, surely, the scene in front of Shun grew hazy, and he collapsed on the spot.

Down in his deep and dreamless sleep, Shun was thinking, *How come people have to die? There's still so much I want to do.* Then, fearfully, Shun opened his eyes to see what had happened. An ancient man in white robes stood before him, and it dawned on Shun that this must be God. In fact, this God was the spitting image of the one Shun had seen at the art museum. *Wow, God, I'd better be on my best behavior.* To pay his respects, Shun leapt to his feet. *Huh? My feet are gone! So ghosts really do float around without any feet.* But then Shun realized something that nearly gave him a heart attack: "It's gone! It's completely gone! My body isn't anywhere!"

This was too much, and Shun lost his head, forgot that he was in the presence of God and started freaking out.

"Oy, oy, oy, there's no need for that," said God. The voice seemed vaguely familiar to Shun, as if he'd heard it long ago. "You'll hardly be needing your body now that you're dead, will you? All the things that used to tie you down and hold you back, they've gone now."

Oh, that's right, yes . . . I'm dead. Despite the fact Shun had no body, all the energy drained right out of it. "Please, sir, what's going to happen to me?"

"Absolutely nothing's going to happen to you, because —well, look around you—you've gone to Heaven."

So what's this place like, exactly? Shun examined his surroundings. The dark was darker than the depths of night, but scattered all about with pulsing stars. *I never saw so many stars where I used to live . . . wow. Stars really are infinite.* Lost in their pure beauty, Shun gazed and gazed, letting thoughts of his death slip away.

"For the time being, do whatever you wish," said God. "I dare say you're still very much attached to your last life, and still have unfinished business to chew over. But you'll come to understand how things stand, by and by." And with that, God's outline began to waver and vanish like mist dissolving into more mist.

It's all very well for Him to say, "Do whatever you wish," Shun thought. He was at a loss. He looked down, and there he saw the Earth, piercingly blue and beautiful in the darkness. *So this here is Space I'm standing in. But what do I do now? How am I supposed to live when I don't even have a body? All alone, as well. The first thing I have to work out is how do you live when you're dead.* Shun had no idea.

For a while, Shun stayed where he was. *This Heaven sure is different than how I used to imagine Heaven would be. I used to think that Heaven was full of wonderful things to eat and fun things to do all day, with nothing to make you suffer or give you a hard time.* Shun shouted out loud: "Hey! What's going on here? Just take me back home, right now!" No sooner had he said this than Shun felt himself hurtling away at a velocity he had never before experienced.

Now where am I? Wait, yes, this is my house. "Mom?" Shun rushed from room to room, looking for his mom. He found her in the Japanese-style room, next to the living room. Shun's heart was pounding. "Mom?" He called her from behind, softly.

She did not turn around for him.

I'm well and truly dead now, aren't I?

Shun's final hope was completely dashed. Downcast, he went around to stand in front of his mom so he could at least take a proper look at her face. She looked so sad and crushed in her black clothes. In his mind, Shun apologized to her. *Mom, I'm so, so sorry I died . . .*

Between Shun and his mom a subtle breeze flowed. Her hand touched his body, the same body she apparently couldn't see because it wasn't there. And Shun felt the same warmth he used to feel back when he was very small, when his mom gave him a cuddle.

Shun's dad came in from the living room. "Hi. What are you doing?"

"Somehow," replied Shun's mom, "I feel Shun's in here."

"Shun's always with us. Always."

Shun wasn't sure quite what to think of this. *I'm dead and gone, but my feelings are the same as they ever were. I want to help Mom and Dad, but there's nothing I can do.* Shun shut his eyes, and in the same instant he was flying away at an astonishing speed.

Shun was back in the place called Heaven. Space was really quiet. All alone, Shun drifted away in his thoughts. He didn't know what to think about himself anymore. He had never imagined that after he died he would be so utterly alone. *I wish there was somebody here I could talk to.* Then he heard something. *What's that sound?* Shun listened, intently. It was a boy's voice. Shun called, "Is there anybody out there?"

"You must be the new one, right? Hi. I'm Kazuo."

Shun was delighted. "Brilliant! I thought there was nobody but me."

"You can't make us out yet, but there are as many people around here as there are stars," said Kazuo. "If you wish it, you'll be able to talk to us—any of us—whenever you want. This world is beyond time, outside of space. Here is perfect freedom. I've been living here in Heaven for eighty years, y'know."

"I don't know what to do here," said Shun. "You say we have perfect freedom, but actually . . . there's nothing here."

Kazuo just laughed. "You ought to do the things you couldn't do when you were still alive." With that, Kazuo slipped away somewhere.

So I ought to do the things I can only do now that I'm dead . . . At that point, numberless lights wrapped around Shun, comforting him like a shimmering blanket. It was like being rocked in a cradle, and at long last, all the tension Shun had felt up to that point began to ebb away. For the first time in many days, Shun fell asleep.

———

Shun was getting used to life in Heaven now, and he had made a lot of friends, as Kazuo had said. Everyone was kind, and there were no barriers of language, ethnicity or era. People lived so peacefully here that it was difficult to believe how much they had fought and quarrelled when they were alive. Shun had never dreamed that owning nothing could be so blissful. He had also, by now, done many of the things that he couldn't during his lifetime. He'd visited every corner of the Earth. He'd spoken with many people in Heaven. Everything was fresh and exciting.

Sometimes Shun visited his parents' home too. It was sad that he couldn't speak with them directly, but it made him happy just to see their faces and listen to them talk about him. This was enough for Shun to stay brave and go on.

It was on a day like this when Shun was visiting his home that his mom looked strange. She was miserable, and didn't seem to be eating. Staring at the photograph of her son, tears were in her eyes. "Shun, I don't think I can go on living like this, without you here. I want to be where you are." Saying this, she collapsed on the table, facedown and weeping.

Shaken, Shun too started to cry. *But I thought she was getting over my death. I thought it was all going to be okay.* "Don't cry, Mom. Mom, please. Don't." Ever so gently, Shun hugged her shoulders. *I'm invisible, she doesn't know I'm here.* Shun's mom kept crying until it got dark, and he stayed by her side.

On his return to Heaven, Shun thought about his parents every single day. *I was sure that at some point things would return to normal for Mom and Dad. But it looks as if their grief will last for the rest of their lives. And although I can be with them, there's nothing I can do to help them.* Shun was sinking into despair. *Well, there's nothing else for it. It's time I asked God for help.* Shun called out in a loud voice: "God? I've got a favor to ask!"

Shimmering out of the mist, God materialized. "I believe you called."

"My parents are still mourning my death, but there's nothing I can do for them, and it's just . . . unbearable."

God nodded as he listened. "Well, I do understand how you must be feeling. Thing is, that's life, isn't it? But your mom and dad will be able to see you again here, when their own numbers are up."

Shun understood God's words, but he still didn't feel any

better. "It's too much for my parents to bear, though. And it's impossible for me to live happily here in Heaven, knowing the pain that my parents are going through!" Shun found he was almost shouting.

"Mmm . . . it is a tricky one. Nowhere's as pleasant as Heaven . . ." God was deep in thought. "Well, I'm not saying there *isn't* a way to help your parents." He then told Shun something quite unexpected. "Namely, being born to your parents as their child once again."

Hearing this, Shun's heart leapt with joy. "Really? Can you honestly do that?" His voice was ragged with excitement and his heart beat faster. *If this can really happen, I'll go back to them right now.*

But, as if reading Shun's mind, God quickly went on: "There is, however, one small catch." God looked Shun straight in the eye. "Once you are born, you won't be Shun any longer. All your memories of Shun, of *being* Shun, will cease to exist."

So there won't be any Me anymore. Shun's hopes withered. *My existence will be wiped out, forever.* Now Shun understood a bit better why Kazuo and his other friends were staying on so long in Heaven. *So what do I do?* Shun wavered. *If I'm not going to be myself anymore, what's the point of being reborn?*

From Heaven, Shun stared down at the blue Earth.

A whole month had passed, but Shun still hadn't made up his mind. He hadn't gone back home, not even once. Life in Heaven suited Shun well, and the thought that he would be seeing his parents here someday gave him a degree of comfort. *Time will sort out everything,* Shun had started to believe.

By and by, a year went by since Shun had died.

On the following Sunday, Shun revisited his old home for the first time in a long time. His mom wasn't in the house, however. He was wondering whether she had gone out shopping when the phone rang. Shun's dad came to answer it. "I see," he said, "I'll be right over."

Shun's dad's voice was an empty husk. He dashed out of the house and Shun followed, with an ominous feeling.

. . . They arrived at the hospital. Shun's dad wore a grim look. *Mom's been hospitalized?* Shun entered her room and gasped with surprise. *Can this really be my mom?*

Lying on the hospital bed was a wrung-out and sickly-pale Mom. She almost looked like a stranger. Shun's dad, too, looked utterly exhausted.

No way! How can Mom have ended up like this?

Shun himself was too gutted to make a sound. *When we all lived together, Mom used to be so cheerful, so bright. This was appalling.*

The doctor concluded his examination and spoke. "Based on her current condition," he said, "I'm afraid there's no guarantee that she'll pull through."

Before the doctor had even finished, Shun rushed up to his mom and shouted, "Mom, you mustn't die yet! Don't die! Please, please, please! Just . . . *don't!*" But his voice couldn't reach where she was. *No, this is too much to take. Even if we met in Heaven, this woman here isn't the same Mom I used to love.*

Even though Shun's mom couldn't hear his voice, in her delirium she called out his name. *"I want to see Shun . . . Shun . . . Shun . . ."*

Shun couldn't bear the pain anymore. It was strangling him, almost. *I thought we could both cope with being separated so long as our hearts stayed connected, but you've lost your spirit and your will to live, haven't you, Mom?* His heart was being torn down the middle. *It's me who caused this grief, so it's me who has to help her now. If I don't do what I can, she's going to die of a broken heart.*

Shun made up his mind.

The future is a thing we build.

He summoned up every ounce of courage, but spoke calmly: "Please, God, I want you to return me to my mother."

In the air, many-colored orbs appeared, and inside each one was a tiny gold sphere. Then, before Shun's eyes, one by one, the orbs popped . . .

Chiming . . .

Chiming . . .

Chiming . . .

Shun thought he recognized the bell-like sound, from a long, long time ago.

In her hospital room, Shun's mother woke up from her sleep.

Shun's father was anxious: "How are you feeling?"

But she didn't make any reply.

"Look, if you're feeling bad, I'll fetch the doctor."

But just as he was about to hurry off, Shun's mother opened her mouth to speak: "Shun came to see me . . . in my dream."

Shun's father held her hand. "That's nice, love."

She went on, with tears in her eyes, "Shun told me, 'I'm right here, always, so you're not to cry anymore, okay?' He looked terribly unhappy, because of, because of the state I'm in. I need to pick myself up, and, and . . . put all the pieces back together again."

Shun's father nodded. "Yes. Shun *is* always watching over us. Let's . . . somehow . . . begin again. Make a fresh start."

At the window, the first snow of the year was falling lightly. The snow crystals had formed from Shun's tears, and were God's proof that a boy called Shun had once lived in this world.

"Look," said Shun's mother. "It's snowing. It's beautiful."

"First snow," said Shun's father. "He always did love the snow, didn't he?"

Five years came and went. As had been promised, in the year after Shun's decision, a new baby had arrived in Shun's family. She was a girl, and was named "Nozomi" to signify "Hope." Nozomi was due to start kindergarten that spring.

"Hang on, Nozomi!" her mom called out. "Wait for me!"

"I'll run ahead a bit, Mommy," Nozomi called back as she ran. *Mommy walks so slowly. As soon as I get to the supermarket, first thing I'll do is to buy some chocolate.* She ran on without looking where she was going, and bumped into someone. "Oh! I'm very sorry," said Nozomi.

"Are you okay?" asked a man in a red hat. "Hey, you're the one who . . ."

"Do you know me?" asked Nozomi, curiously. "Who are you?"

The man hunkered down on his heels: "Are you back here already? This here old man's an angel, believe it or not."

Nozomi thought this was a bit suspect, because angels are supposed to have wings and live in Heaven. "Oh no you're not." She stared back at the old man with her big round eyes.

A cheerful laugh escaped him. "Anyway, are you having a content enough life?"

What does "a content life" mean anyway? Nozomi had to think about this. *Mommy and Daddy quite often say, "We're having a pretty content life." So yes, I must be having a content life too.* Nozomi beamed at the old man. "Of course I am."

Finally, Nozomi's mom caught up with her daughter, out of breath. "What are you up to now?"

"Talking to him." Nozomi turned back, but there was nobody there. "Oh. Where did he go?" Nozomi looked around. "There was this funny old man . . . he said he was an angel."

"I've told you not to talk to strangers," Nozomi's mom said, a little sharply.

So that old man was a stranger? Nozomi's heart went taut with a sort of joy. *What's this I'm feeling now?*

"Anyway," said her mother. "Let's get on with the shopping, shall we?"

Oh yes, the chocolate. "Mommy, can you buy some chocolate? One bar for me and one for my brother, so that'll be two bars, please."

"All right, all right. But you're going to scoff them both down, I bet."

"That's because he says I can have his."

"Lucky you to have such a nice brother."

On their way back from the supermarket, Nozomi's mom was thinking about Shun. *One day, in the future, I'll see Shun again. Until that day, I'll manage. I'll manage just fine.*

Nozomi started running off again. "Mommy! Let's go

and see the cherry trees that my brother used to love." *The things my brother used to like are the same things that I like.* Gazing at the cherry blossoms, Nozomi wondered what sort of a person Shun was.

Afterword

What am I going to be, if my autism can never be cured? When I was little, this question was always a big, big worry. I used to be afraid that as long as I had autism, I'd never be able to live properly as a human being. There were so many things I couldn't do like other people, and having to apologize day in, day out totally drained me of hope.

I hope that by reading my explanations about autism and its mysteries, you can come to understand that all the obstacles that present themselves don't come from our selfishness or from ego. If all of you can grasp this truth about us, we are handed a ray of hope. However hard an autistic life is, however sad it can be, so long as there's hope we can stick at it.

And when the light of hope shines on all this world, then our future will be connected with your future. That's what I want, above all.

A Note from the Illustrators

The Reason I Jump connected with us on a number of levels, but most overwhelmingly Naoki's relationship with nature was the link for the imagery. Naoki returns to nature again and again in the book. He can see beauty and meaning within nature and abstract this information and relate it back to himself, and always turns to nature for comfort and refers to it as his friend. We use nature in our work to connect with people, to provoke thoughts and memories. We like the idea of showing something you can't actually see—and asking bigger questions. We use nature-based images as a metaphor for other feelings. For us, this was how we could combine our imagery with Naoki and his powerful story.

The book was extremely moving for us and we found the way Naoki sees the world, despite his difficulties, inspiring.

Kai and Sunny

The Reason
I Jump

Naoki Higashida

A
READER'S
GUIDE

A Postscript

___

DAVID MITCHELL

During the run-up to the publication of Naoki Higashida's *The Reason I Jump* in English, I had certain
hopes but no solid expectations. My hopes were that if
we were lucky perhaps a few thousand copies would be
printed in the U.K. and in North America, and that these
would find the parents, relatives, and siblings of people
with autism and provide insight into what life inside an
autistically wired head is like, and that more fruitful in-
teraction might grow from that insight. I hoped that the
neurotypical reader of *Jump* might understand that even
people with severe autism can possess an acute intellect
and a fertile imagination. I hoped that with access to
Naoki's never-ending struggle with the speechlessness of
his autism, perhaps a few more "autism outsiders" might
view the neuro-atypical as heroes worthy of respect who

can and should contribute to the human story, rather than as genetic losers worthy of pity at best, or as burdens on welfare budgets or school resources at worst. Finally, I hoped that the book's publication might persuade a few more people that to use the adjective "autistic" as a synonym for "self-obsessed," "inward-looking," or "emotionally anal" is not urbane and snazzy but demeaning, ignorant, and wrongheaded. That was pretty much it.

If I'd been told that *The Reason I Jump* would muscle its way to the top of bestseller charts on both sides of the Atlantic and roost there for several weeks, I would have been highly dubious—but this is what happened. It may be that my own niche profile as a novelist helped earn *Jump* a bit of extra attention in the clamorous marketplace of worthy books, and it's a surer bet that a superb radio dramatization by BBC Radio 4's Allegra McIlroy and a glowing endorsement by *The Daily Show*'s influential Jon Stewart earned the book a lot more notice, but any publisher will affirm that attention alone is no guarantee of the readership *The Reason I Jump* has found, numbering well into six figures so far. A book can achieve such sales only on its own merits. Nor was I expecting so many translations of *Jump* into other languages—this insider's guide to the autistic experience by a Japanese thirteen-year-old, first published in 2007, has, at the time of writing, been translated into twenty-four languages (with more on the way), from Chinese to Macedonian. Naoki Higashida, to the best of my knowledge, is now the most widely translated living Japanese author after Haruki Murakami.

When I met Naoki in a conference room in a Tokyo hotel in March 2014, it was hard to be certain whether the worldwide success his book is enjoying had sunk in, or whether he was just taking it all in stride. Japan's state broadcaster, NHK, was filming the occasion, but even factoring in the presence of the TV crew, Naoki's struggle to communicate through the barrier of autism and to combat the myriad distractions it caused was constant, valiant, and humbling. He needed several attempts to sit down opposite me and begin our talk. Generally, the interview took the form of my asking questions, directly or through an interpreter, and Naoki's answering them by tapping out his answers, letter by letter, on a *"moji-ban"* or cardboard keyboard like the one described at the beginning of The Reason I Jump. Naoki voiced each letter as he touched it, and in this way built up long and thoughtful answers to my questions. It wasn't all plain sailing— sometimes he would lose his way and have to start over again, sometimes he would get distracted by a jingle or a phrase that was occupying his head that day, and sometimes his train of thought would get hijacked by an anxiety about what time he'd be going home or when we would break for lunch, as if he was concerned about being lost in time. I remembered a sniffy American review of *Jump* as well as a British commentator who had concluded that the author of such eloquent sentences couldn't be "severely" autistic and must have high-functioning Asperger's or (more bizarrely) locked-in syndrome instead, and I wished they could have witnessed firsthand the severity of the autism-derived blocks that Naoki was overcoming to communicate with me.

Apart from his phrasal tics and his voicings of the letters he was tapping, Naoki was pretty much nonoral throughout, only once or twice managing a direct spoken answer to a yes/no question; the *moji-ban* is a much-needed handrail, mind map, and concentrator of thought. The gap, however, between what you see and what you get—the gap between a young man whose every waking second is in thrall to his neuro-atypical wiring and the thoughts that he is capable of articulating—is pronounced, and to an "autism-outsider" astonishing. It affirms what is to me the single most important aspect of *The Reason I Jump*: that we neurotypicals are constantly underestimating the intellectual and imaginative potential of people with autism.

Naoki and I discussed autism, the workings of the mind, and the art of writing, and when the cameras were off we talked about our families and our lives, and I showed him video clips of my son on my iPhone. Our conversation, tiring and hard-won as it was for my new writer friend, was one of the most nutritious of my life, and I'll treasure it until my last breath.

A Conversation Between
David Mitchell and Andrew Solomon

———

Andrew Solomon is the author of several books, including *Far from the Tree* and *The Noonday Demon*. He lives in London and New York with his husband and children.

Andrew Solomon: Why do you think that such narratives from inside autism are so rare—and what do you think allowed Naoki Higashida to find a voice?

David Mitchell: Autism comes in a bewildering and shifting array of shapes, severities, colors, and sizes, as you of all writers know, Dr. Solomon, but the common denominator is a difficulty in communication. Naturally, this will impair the ability of a person with autism to compose narratives, for the same reason that deaf composers are thin on the ground, or blind portraitists. While not belittling the Herculean work Naoki and his tutors and parents did when he was learning to type, I also think he got a lucky genetic/neural break: The manifestation of Naoki's autism just happens to be of a type that (a) permitted a cogent communicator to develop behind his initial speechlessness, and (b) then did not entomb this communicator by preventing him from writing. This combination appears to be rare.

AS: What, in your view, is the relationship between language and intelligence? How do autistic people who have no expressive language best manifest their intelligence?

DM: It would be unwise to describe a relationship between two abstract nouns without having a decent intellectual grip on what those nouns mean. Language, sure, the way in which we communicate; but intelligence is to definition what Teflon is to warm cooking oil. I feel most at home in the school that talks about "intelligences" rather than intelligence in the singular, whereby each is a fuzzy cluster of aptitudes: numerical, emotional, logical, abstract, artistic, "common sense"—and linguistic. In this model, language is one subset of intelligence—and, *Homo sapiens* being the communicative, cooperative bunch that we are, rather a crucial one, for without linguistic intelligence it's hard to express (or even verify the existence of) the other types. I guess that people with autism who have no expressive language manifest their intelligence the same way you would if duct tape were put over your mouth and a *Men in Black*–style memory zapper removed your ability to write: by identifying problems and solving them. *I want a choccie biccie, but the cookie jar's too high: I'll get the stool and stand on it.* Or, *Dad's telling me I have to have my socks on before I can play on his iPhone, but I'd rather be barefoot: I'll pull the tops of my socks over my toes, so he can't say they aren't on, then I'll get the iPhone.* Or, *This game needs me to add 7+4: I'll input 12, no, that's no good, try 11, yep. . . .*

AS: Naoki Higashida comes off as very charming, but describes being very difficult for his parents. Do you think that the slightly self-mocking humor he shows will give him an easier life than he'd have had without the charm?

DM: Definitely. Humor is a delightful sensation, and an antidote to many ills. I feel that it is linked to wisdom, but I'm neither wise nor funny enough to have ever worked out quite how they intertwine.

AS: As you translated this book from the Japanese, did you feel you could represent Naoki's voice much as it was in his native language? Did you find that there are Japanese ways of thinking that required as much translation from you and your wife as autistic ways required of the author?

DM: Our goal was to write the book as Naoki would have done if he were a thirteen-year-old British kid with autism, rather than a thirteen-year-old Japanese kid with autism. Once we had identified that goal, many of the 1,001 choices you make while translating became clear. Phrasal and lexical repetition is less of a vice in Japanese—it's almost a virtue—so varying Naoki's phrasing while keeping the meaning was a ball we had to keep our eyes on. Linguistic directness can come over as vulgar in Japanese, but this is more of a problem when Japanese is the "into" language than when it is the "out of" language. The only other regular head-bender is the rendering of onomatopoeia, for which Japanese has a synesthetic genius—not just animal sounds, but qualities of light, or texture, or motion. Those puzzles were fun, though.

AS: Higashida has written dreamlike stories that punctuate the narrative. Can you say what functional or narrative purpose they serve in the book?

DM: Their inclusion was, I guess, an idea of the book's original Japanese editor, for whom I can't speak. But for me they provide little coffee breaks from the Q&A, as well as showing that Naoki can write creatively and in slightly different styles. The story at the end is an attempt to show us neurotypicals what it would feel like if we couldn't communicate. The story is, in a way, *The Reason I Jump* but reframed and rehung in fictional form. They also prove that Naoki is capable of metaphor and analogy.

AS: The book came out in its original form in Japan some years ago. Do you know what has happened to the author since the book was published?

DM: Naoki has had a number of other books about autism published in Japan, both prior to and after *Jump*. He's now about twenty, and he's doing okay. He receives invitations to talk about autism at various universities and institutions throughout Japan. This involves his reading a presentation aloud and taking questions from the audience, which he answers by typing. This isn't easy for him, but he usually manages okay. In terms of public knowledge about autism, Europe is a decade behind the States, and Japan's about a decade behind us, and Naoki would view his role as that of an autism advocate, to close that gap. (I happen to know that in Hiroshima, for instance, a city of well over a million people, there isn't a single doctor qualified to give a diagnosis of autism.)

AS: Many people would presume that Naoki's autism can't be very severe if he could write such a book—but I think that "severity" is a troubled concept. How would you assess this?

DM: Since the U.K. publication, this is the question (or question mark) that I've had to tackle most often, and perhaps the question that I've learned the most from. Naoki's first tentative diagnosis, at the age of four, was "autistic tendencies," just like my own son's. Psychiatrists are unwilling and unable to commit, and tend to understate the severity of the autism that these startled, scared, rabbit-in-the-headlights parents sitting across the desk are going to have to handle. They must feel like judges handing down life sentences, and the exact terms of those sentences. Their motives may be benign, if misplaced, but that's another topic. More recent diagnoses have described Naoki's autism as "severe"—this term is on his books in Japan, too—but I've come to realize how vexingly subjective the severity spectrum within ASD is. You can see Naoki at about age sixteen in Gerardine

Wurzburg's fine documentary *Wretches and Jabberers*, where it is clear that having any kind of a sustained spoken dialogue is pretty much impossible for him—communication has to be by keyboard or it won't really happen. Naoki displays many of the classic symptoms of autism (but not all, and nobody does) and is still subject to panic attacks and meltdowns; mainstream schooling was impossible, independent living is impossible, and while he can address an audience in Kumamoto, if he were left alone outside the lecture theater he would be in severe trouble severely soon.

Compared to a kid with Asperger's who gets by fine in an ordinary classroom with a bit of SNA attention, Naoki's autism is most certainly severe. And yet compared to some of the "Welcome to Beirut" cases you describe in *Far from the Tree*, he has gotten off lightly. I was attacked on "Woman's Hour" on Radio 4 recently by someone whose son's autism sounds much harder to live with than either Naoki's or my son's, and who said nobody with "severe" autism could use a keyboard, let alone use metaphor. What I was too slow-witted to say in response was that autism isn't a fixed point on a ruler from *mild* to *severe*, that autism's multiplex nature pretty much dooms any attempts to quantify it from the outset. In my experience, people with autism exhibit only mild symptoms in some areas, but severe symptoms in others and at different times. As it happens, Naoki has developed methods to overcome the block on his ability to communicate, so in this area his autism doesn't look severe, but in other areas it does. What do you do with this? How do you describe the autism? Are you actually measuring it, or the degree to which the individual has or hasn't been able to integrate coping mechanisms into behavior? I don't have the answers, but I wish the narrative could move beyond people wanting a single adjective like "severe" or "mild," as if autism were a cold. It feels lazy somehow, and if you're the one with autism, any degree of severity must feel overwhelmingly severe many times per day.

Questions for Discussion

———

1. What do you think it is about *The Reason I Jump* that has caught the imagination of general narrative non-fiction and fiction fans and made it appeal beyond readers with a particular interest in autism, such as parents and carers of children with autism?

2. Nature is a recurring theme throughout the book. Why do you think nature is so important to Naoki and other children with autism and how does he demonstrate this?

3. How does the book deal with the issue of what is "normal"? Did it make you reconsider your own perceptions of what this is?

4. "People with autism have no freedom. The reason is that we are a different kind of human." What does freedom mean to Naoki? Do you agree?

5. This may be the only first-person account of life with autism that many readers have encountered. What did you learn about autism from reading Naoki's book, and do you think the lessons of this book could be applied to people with other illnesses or conditions and their carers?

6. "The hardest ordeal for us is the idea that we are the source of other people's unhappiness." Naoki often returns to his guilt about the impact of his condition on others. What advice would you give Naoki, if you had the chance?

7. Language is a barrier to Naoki's self-expression. Have you ever felt the inadequacy of words to communicate your experiences?

8. The final section of the book is a short story featuring a child narrating from heaven following his death in a car accident. He watches his parents cope with his loss and experiences the helplessness of not being able to provide comfort to his grieving family. In the end, he chooses to go back, reborn in a new body to his mother, losing his memory of who he was before. Naoki explains in the book that he writes short stories to make sense of, or to

help him remember, experiences or emotions. What, then, do you think this particular story represents?

9. This short story is quite unusual in adult publishing, in that it not only features a narrator who is a child but is also written by a child. How do you think this differs from other recent and classic books featuring child narrators, such as Alice Sebold's *The Lovely Bones,* Mark Haddon's *The Curious Incident of the Dog in the Night-Time, Room* by Emma Donoghue, *Extremely Loud and Incredibly Close* by Jonathan Safran Foer, or Harper Lee's *To Kill a Mockingbird*? Also, can we trust the child as narrator, and what do we gain from the story when it is told from this perspective?

10. Are there any other questions you would like to ask Naoki?

TURN THE PAGE

FOR AN EXCERPT FROM

NAOKI HIGASHIDA'S

———

Fall Down 7 Times
Get Up 8

———

AVAILABLE FROM

RANDOM HOUSE

One Army Fighting Hard

There are times when I wonder where this disability called "autism" comes from. Could it have been created, I wonder, by humankind itself? I can't help but feel that some imbalance in this world first caused neuro-atypical people to be needed and then brought into being. This isn't to say that all of us are delighted to be the way we are all the time, of course. But I refuse to accept it when people view us as incomplete or partial human beings; I prefer to believe that people with autism are every bit as whole as anyone else. We might be different from the majority in diverse ways, but why are these differences negative things?

Just as everyone has a heart, so everyone with autism possesses an array of feelings: real, if invisible feelings. Even among people who can speak, shyness or unwilling-ness aren't the only reasons why some don't reveal everything about themselves. To display your emotions is, after all, to put your whole self up for scrutiny. Perhaps total exposure of the self is not even possible. Emotions can be unfathomable things—and therefore hidden, even to the self. Yet emotions—as everyone surely knows—are also what make us human.

Empathy and Endurance

It is often said that we people with autism lack empathy and any understanding of other people's emotions. In my view, however, people with neurotypical brains aren't so fantastic at getting to grips with *our* emotions, either. Anyway, there are times when I can't help but wonder if not being able to divine the inner feelings of the people around us is, in reality, the debilitating problem it's cracked up to be. Shouldn't how we feel inside of ourselves be at least as important? How much use can we really be for other people unless we *first* find the headspace for questions about ourselves—*What are my priorities now?* or *How was I feeling when such-and-such a thing happened?* or *Am I on the right path through life?*—and the answers. Some people with autism might not yet be fully able to understand themselves. Some might not understand others. Some might not wish to *try* to understand. Sometimes a situation occurs when I lose my capacity for patience, even though I fully understand why the situation has come about. Some onlookers might tell me, "You're not patient enough—just show a little endurance!" But how can degrees of patience be measured, exactly? Mastering emotions can be so overwhelmingly taxing that I sometimes wonder, *Am I wholly to blame if I can't handle this?* Our world would improve if the neurotypical majority could try to empathize a little better and a little more often with people like me who "lack endurance."

Loneliness and Autism

The word for "autism" in Japanese—*jiheisho*—conveys an image of people locking themselves up inside themselves. This is misleading. People with autism aren't good at interacting with others, for sure, but our hearts and minds are always open and ready to receive. If we were truly clammed shut inside ourselves, we wouldn't be coming out with our weird utterances or be prone to panic attacks. I take these phenomena as proof that our emotions exist and are trying to exhibit themselves. Some people might not care either way whether the emotions of people with autism are locked away or not, but indifference doesn't help us. The neurotypical public needs to know that the failure of people with autism to communicate doesn't stem from inner self-imprisonment: it stems from a failure of others to see that we are open and receptive. To venture out into the world requires help from other people. Please lend us that support as we strive to live in society.

I always think of the loneliness of nonverbal people with autism as being like the darkness before the dawn. Hope might be just around the corner, but we can't imagine that the night will ever end. In general, people just don't understand how lonely nonverbal people with autism can be. When I stop and think about it, I see that everyone is kind of alone from the day they're born until the moment they die. People with whom we can share *all* our days and thoughts don't actually exist. It's to nullify this essential loneliness that people connect with others, I think . . . Meaning that nonverbal people with autism, who can't make these connections, are probably the loneliest souls of all.

Looking at it another way, however, if we accept the idea that human beings exist in isolation, then we nonverbal people with autism really aren't so unique. Memories remain, equally and evenly, whether you're a solitary person or not. The heart treasures the memory of giving and receiving love, whether you can connect with others via language or not. Maybe we'll only discover whether our lives were truly lonely when we're on our deathbeds.

Some of you might be concerned that people with autism have nobody to share their feelings with. Because we can't talk, it's kind of inevitable that we can't make our innermost feelings known easily, if at all. That might be the sad reality, but I don't think it calls for all-out despair. Why? Because we "nonverbals" have a friend who lives inside us. Inhabiting my mind is a person who is Me and yet isn't Me. I talk to my other me as if he were an old friend, both when I'm happy and when I'm sad. This is why it's especially important never to hate ourselves. Once you start hating yourself, this old companion draws away. It's not easy to maintain your self-esteem if you're constantly feeling removed from your ideal self.

So. Please go ahead and tell us nonverbals "I like you" or "I love you" whenever the fancy takes you. When someone tells you that, it becomes a whole lot easier to like yourself.

Anger

Some people with autism go into a meltdown at the very sight of someone else getting a major scolding. Because of this, neurotypical people arrive at the conclusion that we hate the sight of anyone else getting into trouble and being shouted at. My take on this, however, is that the real reason the person with autism is shaken up so badly is because they are experiencing the scene as one where *they* are getting blamed for their own flaws and defects. I don't mean that he or she is suffering a flashback or that there is any confusion over who is in trouble. Nor do I think that any meltdown is rooted in an inability to help their friend in trouble, or arising from empathy. My theory is that witnessing the anger is a trigger for a panic attack, which then snowballs into a full meltdown as the neuro-atypical on-looker gets trapped in a spiral of self-loathing for having had a panic attack in the first place. Nobody's accusing them of anything at all, but they nonetheless experience blame and suffer the full stress. As for the reason why the person being told off *is* being told off? I suspect it rarely enters the equation.

Laughing

Even when somebody is laughing their head off in front of me, I find it very hard to laugh along with them. It's not that I fail to find what they're laughing at funny: it's that I literally can't do it, because the moment I see someone start laughing, I forget to join in—I become entranced by the sight of the other person's laughing face. Then, when I'm *not* looking at the laughing person, I become ensnared by the *sound* of them laughing. In this way it slips my mind that I ever wanted to laugh. Not being able to laugh while everyone else is falling about the place is isolating enough, but what makes me feel even lonelier is that my inability to laugh along with others leads people to assume that I don't share their feelings or humor.

There are other times when I find the difference between an angry person's face and their normal face utterly hilarious. I might even want to see the furious expression again so badly that I burst out laughing—despite the anger this generates. Over-the-top scoldings definitely backfire in my case.

It can be tricky, I guess, to make people with autism like mine understand why they are being told off, especially when we're very young. The scene in which we did something wrong simply doesn't mesh with the scene in which we're being reprimanded. No doubt it varies from person to person, but I suggest that if a neuro-atypical child has done something wrong, the best course of action is just to point the misdemeanor out. Coolly and calmly.

Thorns in the Heart

When I was a small boy, I used to think I could catch up with everyone else simply by refusing to quit. But as I grew up, I came to understand that, because of my autism, there are some things that other people do which I will never master, no matter how hard I try. The memory of how this realization wounded my spirit remains in my heart like a thorn that cannot be extracted. I assumed this wound would be with me forever because damage done in the past cannot be remedied.

By tackling challenges one by one, however, I've grown to be able to do a number of things that I couldn't do when I was young, and nowadays I'm a lot sunnier. When I was younger only *I* knew how miserable I was and I'd curl up under my stone. People would try to comfort me, telling me, "Hey, it's not such a big deal"—but for me, it really *was* a big deal. These days, however, I can look back at those scenes and agree: no, it wasn't the end of the world. My wrongheadedness caused me to misinterpret what the people watching over me were saying.

It turns out that wounds in the memory *can* be remedied, after all. How great it felt to draw that thorn out of my heart.

Grace

I often cause trouble for other people. This sometimes makes me miserable. But however inconsolable I get, I usually find that by the following day the wound has pretty much healed over. It's thanks to this that I can carry on and function as normal. Whatever it was that had happened, my family just acts as if nothing out of the ordinary had occurred. My family's attitude means that the only thing I need to be concerned about is myself and my attitude. Since I've reached adulthood, I've come to appreciate how lucky I am to live in an environment such as the one my family gives me. While we can often overcome our own hardships, doing something about the troubles of other people is a much taller order. But when I hear the laughter of my family I feel this bubble-like, evanescent sensation— it's like when I'm entranced by a really great picture book I love, set in a distant land, beyond borders. Joyful memories warm my heart even now, like the lullabies heard long ago. They might be buried deep inside me but they're there and they're priceless and life without them would be impossible.

NAOKI HIGASHIDA was born in Kimitsu, Japan, in 1992. Diagnosed with severe autism when he was five, he subsequently learned to communicate using a hand-made alphabet grid and began to write poems and short stories. At the age of thirteen he wrote *The Reason I Jump*, which was published in Japan in 2007. Its English translation came out in 2013, and it has now been published in more than thirty languages. Higashida has since published several books in Japan, including children's and picture books, poems, and essays. A collection of his observations focused on autism in young adulthood, *Fall Down 7 Times Get Up 8*, was published in English in 2017. The subject of an award-winning Japanese television documentary in 2014, Higashida continues to give presentations throughout the country about his experience of autism.

KA YOSHIDA was born in Yamaguchi, Japan, and majored in English poetry at Notre Dame Seishin University.

DAVID MITCHELL is the author of the international bestsellers *Slade House, The Bone Clocks, The Thousand Autumns of Jacob de Zoet, Black Swan Green, Cloud Atlas, Number9Dream,* and *Ghostwritten.*

KA Yoshida and David Mitchell live in Ireland with their two children.

KAI AND SUNNY are a multidisciplinary duo whose work appears in many arenas of art. Their intricate, natural and sometimes sinister style has led them to collaborate with Alexander McQueen and to design the jackets of several of David Mitchell's books, and has won them numerous accolades, including a 2012 D&AD design award. The artists have exhibited internationally, including at Haunch of Venison London, and have recently been included in the Victoria and Albert Museum print archive collection. The duo are currently exploring natural forms in large-scale monotone prints.